W9-AUY-256

EYEWITNESS VISUAL DICTIONARIES

THE VISUAL DICTIONARY *of*

PREHISTORIC LIFE

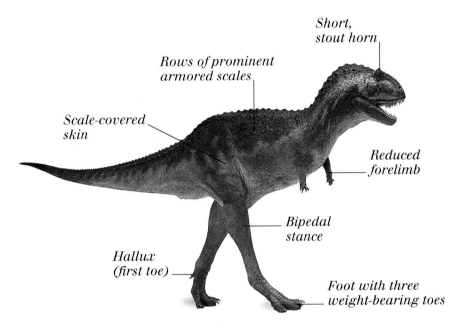

Short, stout horn

Rows of prominent armored scales

Scale-covered skin

Reduced forelimb

Bipedal stance

Hallux (first toe)

Foot with three weight-bearing toes

A LATE CRETACEOUS THEROPOD DINOSAUR
(Carnotaurus sastrei)
Length: 25 ft (7.6 m)

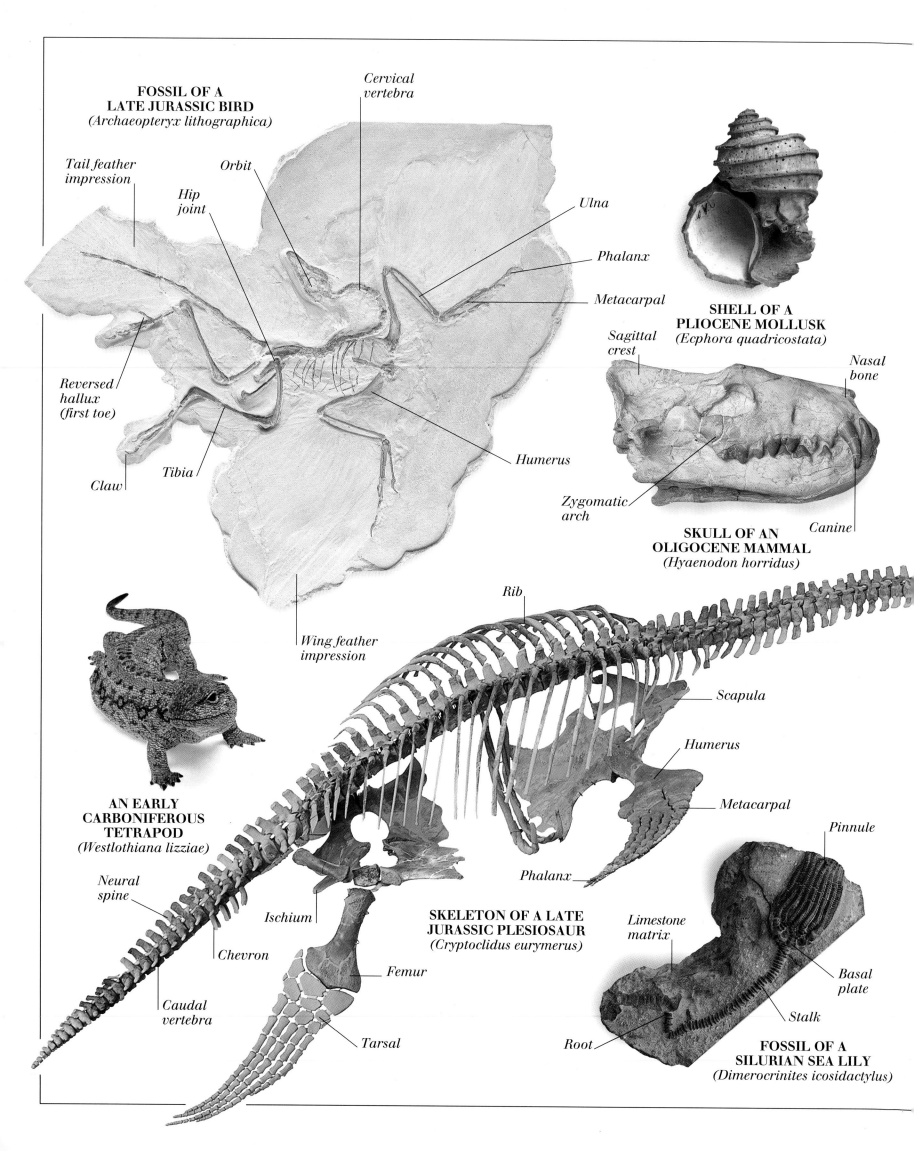

**FOSSIL OF A
LATE JURASSIC BIRD**
(Archaeopteryx lithographica)

Cervical
vertebra

Tail feather
impression

Orbit

Hip
joint

Ulna

Phalanx

Metacarpal

Reversed
hallux
(first toe)

Humerus

Claw

Tibia

Wing feather
impression

**SHELL OF A
PLIOCENE MOLLUSK**
(Ecphora quadricostata)

Sagittal
crest

Nasal
bone

Zygomatic
arch

Canine

**SKULL OF AN
OLIGOCENE MAMMAL**
(Hyaenodon horridus)

Rib

Scapula

Humerus

Metacarpal

Phalanx

**AN EARLY
CARBONIFEROUS
TETRAPOD**
(Westlothiana lizziae)

Neural
spine

Ischium

**SKELETON OF A LATE
JURASSIC PLESIOSAUR**
(Cryptoclidus eurymerus)

Pinnule

Limestone
matrix

Chevron

Femur

Basal
plate

Caudal
vertebra

Tarsal

Stalk

Root

**FOSSIL OF A
SILURIAN SEA LILY**
(Dimerocrinites icosidactylus)

EYEWITNESS VISUAL DICTIONARIES

THE VISUAL
DICTIONARY *of*
PREHISTORIC
LIFE

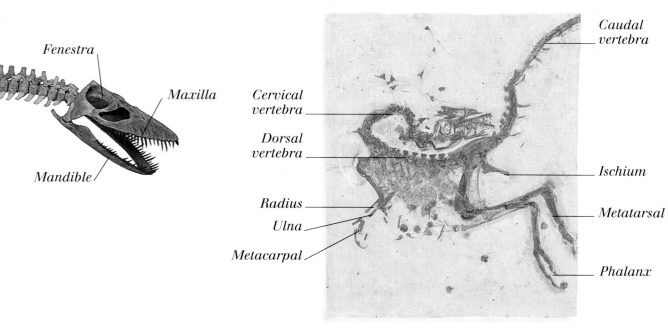

Fenestra

Maxilla

Mandible

Caudal vertebra

Cervical vertebra

Dorsal vertebra

Radius

Ulna

Metacarpal

Ischium

Metatarsal

Phalanx

**SKELETON OF A LATE JURASSIC
THEROPOD DINOSAUR**
(Compsognathus longipes)

DORLING KINDERSLEY
LONDON • NEW YORK • STUTTGART

A DORLING KINDERSLEY BOOK

Art Editor Johnny Pau
Project Editor Edward Bunting
Editorial Assistant Will Hodgkinson

US Editor Jill Hamilton
US Consultants Elana Benamy, Ted Daeschler

Consultant Editor David Lambert
Botanical Consultant Barry Thomas

Managing Art Editor Philip Gilderdale
Managing Editor Ruth Midgley

Illustrations John Temperton, Coral Mula, Deborah Maizels, Colin Rose
Picture Research Sharon Southren
Production Hilary Stephens

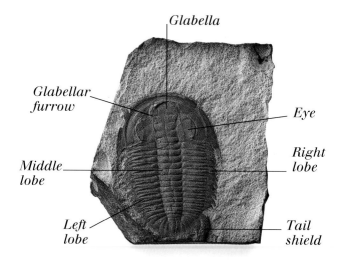

Glabella

Glabellar furrow

Eye

Middle lobe

Right lobe

Left lobe

Tail shield

MIDDLE CAMBRIAN TRILOBITE
(Xystridura saint-smithii)

First American Edition, 1995

2 4 6 8 10 9 7 5 3 1

Published in the United States by Dorling Kindersley Publishing, Inc.,
95 Madison Avenue, New York, New York 10016

Copyright © 1995
Dorling Kindersley Limited, London

All rights reserved under International and Pan-American Copyright Conventions.
No part of this publication may be reproduced, stored in a retrieval system, or transmitted
in any form or by any means, electronic, mechanical, photocopying, recording, or otherwise,
without the prior written permission of the copyright owner. Published in Great Britain
by Dorling Kindersley Limited.
Distributed by Houghton Mifflin Company, Boston.

Library of Congress Cataloging-in-Publication Data
The visual dictionary of prehistoric life. — 1st American ed.
p. cm. — (Eyewitness visual dictionaries)
Includes index.
ISBN 1–56458–859–9
1. Man, Prehistoric—Juvenile literature. 2. Animals, Fossil—Juvenile literature.
3. Plants, Fossil—Juvenile literature. 4. Dinosaurs—Juvenile literature. I. Series.
GN744.V57 1995
560—dc20   94–30705
                                                CIP
                                                AC

Reproduced by Colourscan, Singapore
Printed and bound by Arnoldo Mondadori in Verona, Italy

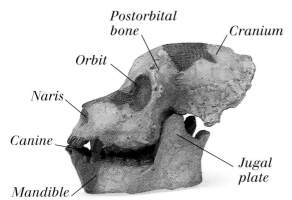

EOCENE HORSE
(Hyracotherium sp.)

*Brow
horn core*

*Nose
horn core*

Neck frill

**SKULL OF A CRETACEOUS
DINOSAUR** *(Triceratops horridus)*

*Alternate
arrangement
of leaflets*

*Pinna
(leaflet)*

Rachis

TRIASSIC CYCAD LEAF
(Cycas sp.)

*Squamosal
bone*

Naris

Orbit

*Incomplete
backbone*

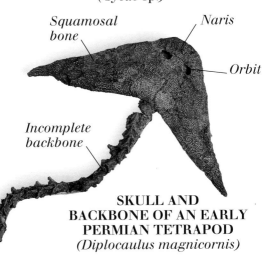

**SKULL AND
BACKBONE OF AN EARLY
PERMIAN TETRAPOD**
(Diplocaulus magnicornis)

Contents

PREHISTORIC TIME 6

PRECAMBRIAN TIME 8

THE PALEOZOIC ERA 10

THE MESOZOIC ERA 12

THE CENOZOIC ERA 14

SPORE-BEARING PLANTS 16

GYMNOSPERMS 18

FLOWERING PLANTS 20

EARLY INVERTEBRATES 22

MOLLUSKS AND BRACHIOPODS 24

ECHINODERMS AND ARTHROPODS 26

PRIMITIVE FISHES 28

THE RISE OF MODERN FISHES 30

THE RISE OF AMPHIBIANS 32

PRIMITIVE AND SYNAPSID REPTILES 34

MARINE REPTILES 36

RELATIVES OF THE DINOSAURS 38

SAURISCHIAN DINOSAURS 40

ORNITHISCHIAN DINOSAURS 42

THE EARLIEST BIRDS 44

PRIMITIVE MAMMALS 46

CARNIVOROUS MAMMALS 48

HOOFED MAMMALS 50

ELEPHANTS AND THEIR KIN 52

PRIMATES 54

TIME CHART: ANIMALS 56

TIME CHART: PLANTS 58

INDEX 59

ACKNOWLEDGMENTS 64

*Postorbital
bone*

Cranium

Orbit

Naris

Canine

*Jugal
plate*

Mandible

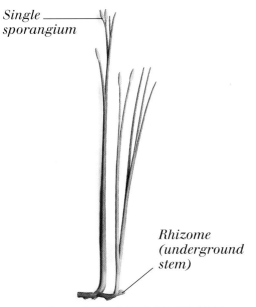

**SKULL OF AN
OLIGOCENE PRIMATE**
(Aegyptopithecus sp.)

*Single
sporangium*

*Rhizome
(underground
stem)*

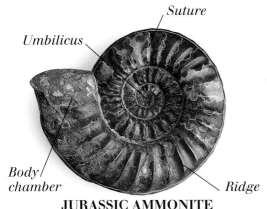

DEVONIAN VASCULAR PLANT
(Aglaophyton sp.)

Suture

Umbilicus

*Body
chamber*

Ridge

JURASSIC AMMONITE
(Asteroceras obtusum)

Frontal bone

Cranium

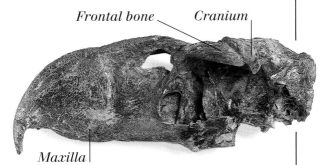

Maxilla

SKULL OF A MIOCENE BIRD
(Phorusracus inflatus)

Prehistoric time

THE PASSAGE OF GEOLOGICAL TIME is marked by the slow formation of sedimentary rocks. These are made over millions of years by the gradual laying down of particles such as dust or sand. The Earth's crust has accumulated thick layers of these rocks, with the oldest at the bottom and the newest on top. In many places, the sequence has been tilted, bent, or otherwise disrupted by geological movement, bringing old rocks to the surface, and with them fossils. The study of prehistoric life begins with the identification of rock formations and fossils, and a necessary part of this is to determine their position in the geological timescale. This timescale divides the history of the Earth into three eons. The Archean eon (4–2.5 billion years ago) began with the formation of the planet and encompassed the time (as yet far from precisely known) when life began, in the form of prokaryotes (organisms without cell nuclei). The Proterozoic eon (2,500–550 million years ago) included the time when eukaryotes (organisms with cell nuclei) appeared. It extended until the time when the Cambrian rocks were laid down. At the start of the Proterozoic, the only living things were bacteria, but by the end there were multicellular plants and animals, all of which lived in water. The Phanerozoic eon (550 million years ago to the present) is the time during which many-celled organisms have dominated life on Earth. The Phanerozoic comprises the Paleozoic, Mesozoic, and Cenozoic eras (see pp. 10–15). The eras are divided into periods, many of which in turn are divided into epochs.

UNCLASSIFIED LATE PROTEROZOIC FOSSIL
(*Mawsonites spriggi*)

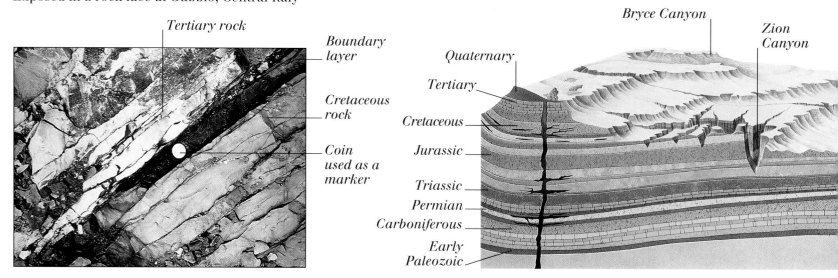

CAMBRIAN PERIOD
(*550–505 mya*)

ORDOVICIAN PERIOD
(*505–438 mya*)

PRECAMBRIAN
(*4,600–550 mya*)

FORMATION OF THE EARTH

SILURIAN PERIOD
(*438–408 mya*)

THE CRETACEOUS/TERTIARY BOUNDARY
Exposed in a rock face at Gubbio, Central Italy

Tertiary rock

Boundary layer

Cretaceous rock

Coin used as a marker

Bryce Canyon

Zion Canyon

Quaternary

Tertiary

Cretaceous

Jurassic

Triassic

Permian

Carboniferous

Early Paleozoic

THE GEOLOGICAL TIMESCALE
MILLIONS OF YEARS AGO (MYA)

4,600	3,500		2,900	2,500	1,600	900	550	505	438

							CAMBRIAN	ORDOVICIAN
			PRECAMBRIAN TIME					

EARLY ARCHEAN	MIDDLE ARCHEAN	LATE ARCHEAN	EARLY PROTEROZOIC	MIDDLE PROTEROZOIC	LATE PROTEROZOIC		
ARCHEAN			PROTEROZOIC				

GEOLOGICAL PERIODS IN EARTH HISTORY

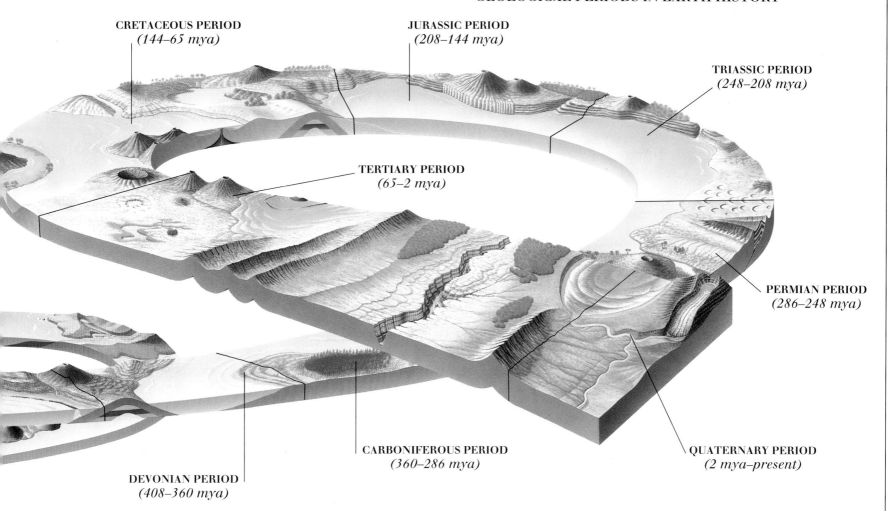

CRETACEOUS PERIOD
(144–65 mya)

JURASSIC PERIOD
(208–144 mya)

TRIASSIC PERIOD
(248–208 mya)

TERTIARY PERIOD
(65–2 mya)

PERMIAN PERIOD
(286–248 mya)

DEVONIAN PERIOD
(408–360 mya)

CARBONIFEROUS PERIOD
(360–286 mya)

QUATERNARY PERIOD
(2 mya–present)

THE GRAND CANYON REGION, UTAH TO ARIZONA
Approximate correlation of rock formations with the geological timescale

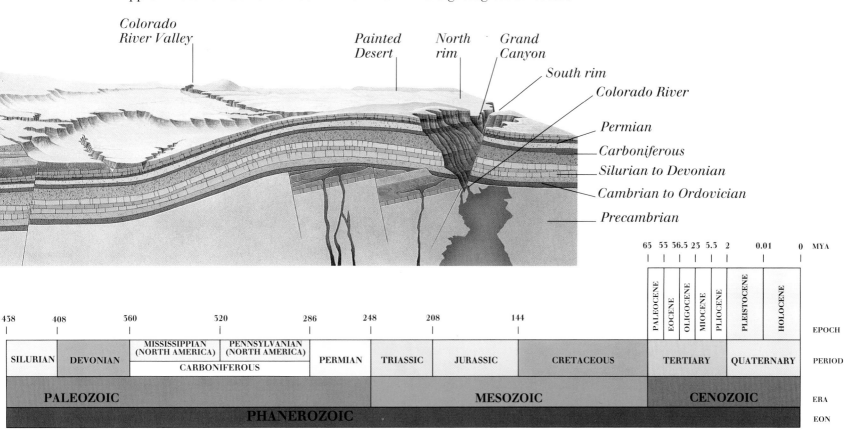

Colorado River Valley

Painted Desert

North rim

Grand Canyon

South rim

Colorado River

Permian

Carboniferous

Silurian to Devonian

Cambrian to Ordovician

Precambrian

| 65 | 53 | 36.5 | 25 | 5.5 | 2 | 0.01 | 0 | MYA |

													PALEOCENE	EOCENE	OLIGOCENE	MIOCENE	PLIOCENE	PLEISTOCENE	HOLOCENE	EPOCH

438	408	360	320	286	248	208	144					

SILURIAN	DEVONIAN	MISSISSIPPIAN (NORTH AMERICA)	PENNSYLVANIAN (NORTH AMERICA)	PERMIAN	TRIASSIC	JURASSIC	CRETACEOUS	TERTIARY	QUATERNARY	PERIOD
		CARBONIFEROUS								

PALEOZOIC	MESOZOIC	CENOZOIC	ERA

PHANEROZOIC	EON

Precambrian time

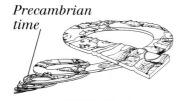

Precambrian time

OVERVIEW OF PREHISTORIC TIME

PRECAMBRIAN TIME ACCOUNTS FOR OVER seven-eighths of the history of the Earth. No sedimentary rocks from the first 800 million years have been found, all of these having apparently been lost through geological change. Sediments 3.8 billion years old have been found in Greenland, and these contain chemicals that indicate the presence of life. The first living things were bacteria, which are classified as prokaryotes—organisms without a cell nucleus. It seems reasonable to place the time of their first appearance at around 3.9 billion years ago, about a third of the way through the Archean eon (4.6–2.5 billion years ago). For the rest of the Archean, prokaryotes were the only living things. The next landmark in evolution, about 1.5 billion years ago, was the arrival of eukaryotes: living things that possess a cell nucleus. This occurred roughly halfway through the Proterozoic eon (2.5–550 million years ago). The first eukaryotes were single-celled algae. These, together with protozoans (another form of single-celled eukaryote), make up the kingdom of protists. Taken altogether, the eukaryotes form an enormous superkingdom which contains four entire kingdoms of the living world—protists, plants, fungi, and animals. Multicellular algae, the first plants, appeared some 1 billion years ago. Fossils of Precambrian animals have been found in the Ediacara Hills of Australia (and elsewhere since then). It is not certain that all of these are fossils of animals; some, such as *Mawsonites* (see p. 6), are so unfamiliar that experts disagree on how to classify them.

MICROGRAPHS OF SINGLE-CELLED EUKARYOTES

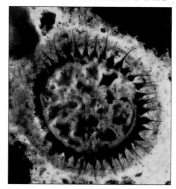

PROTEROZOIC PROTIST
Probably the cyst of an alga, 580 million years old

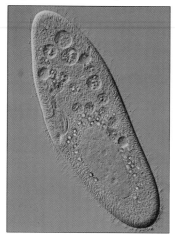

LIVING PROTIST
A complex protozoan (*Paramecium* sp.)

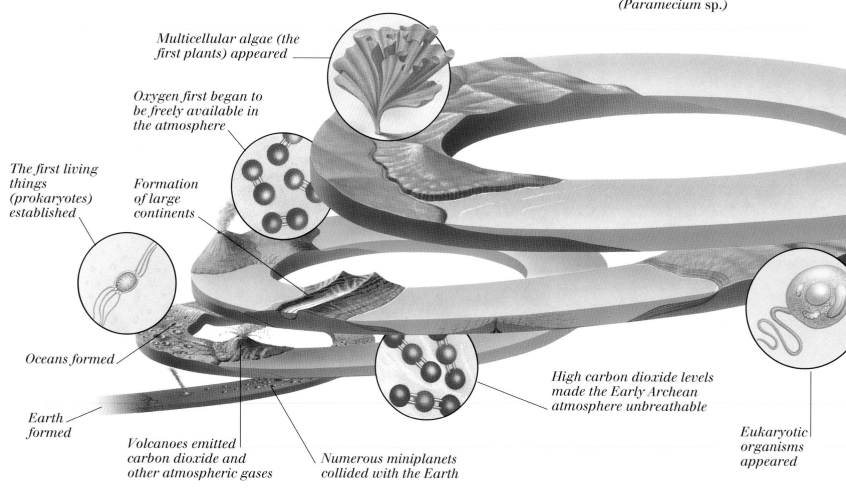

Multicellular algae (the first plants) appeared

Oxygen first began to be freely available in the atmosphere

The first living things (prokaryotes) established

Formation of large continents

Oceans formed

Earth formed

Volcanoes emitted carbon dioxide and other atmospheric gases

Numerous miniplanets collided with the Earth

High carbon dioxide levels made the Early Archean atmosphere unbreathable

Eukaryotic organisms appeared

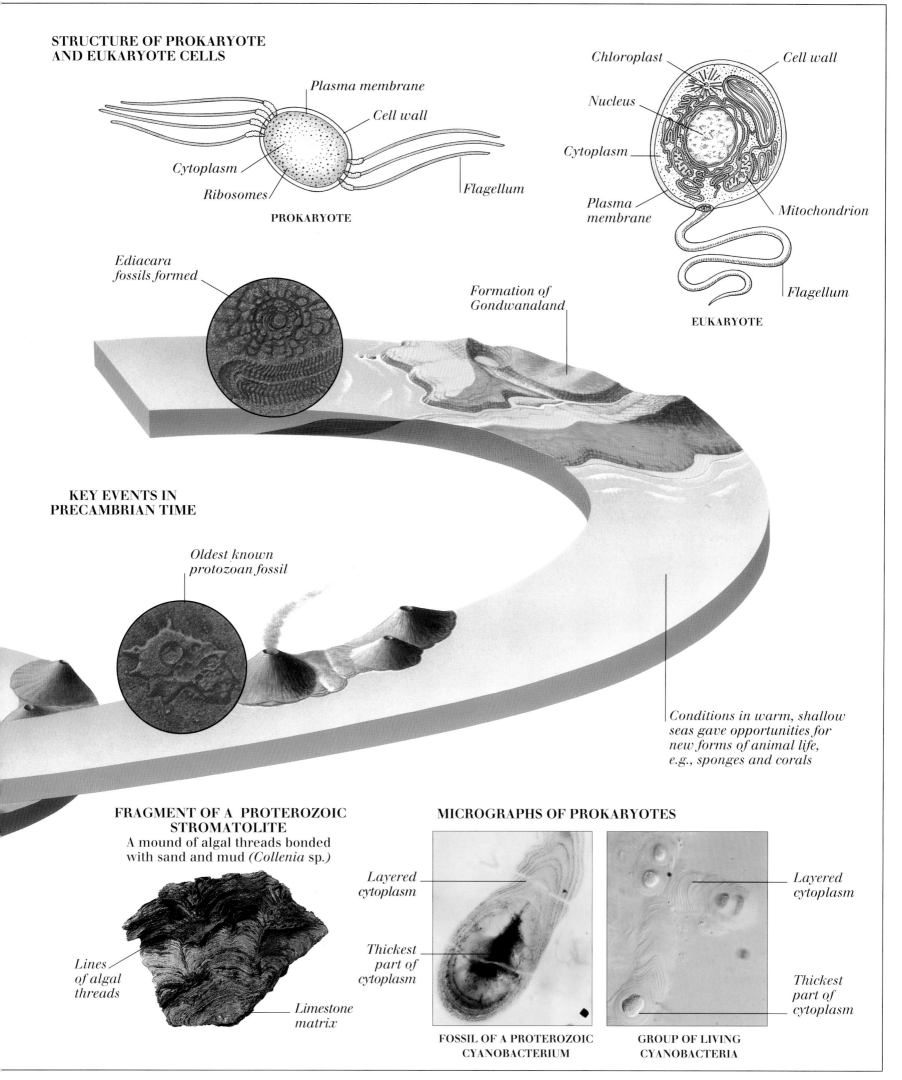

STRUCTURE OF PROKARYOTE AND EUKARYOTE CELLS

Plasma membrane

Cell wall

Cytoplasm

Ribosomes

PROKARYOTE

Flagellum

Chloroplast

Cell wall

Nucleus

Cytoplasm

Plasma membrane

Mitochondrion

Flagellum

EUKARYOTE

Ediacara fossils formed

Formation of Gondwanaland

KEY EVENTS IN PRECAMBRIAN TIME

Oldest known protozoan fossil

Conditions in warm, shallow seas gave opportunities for new forms of animal life, e.g., sponges and corals

FRAGMENT OF A PROTEROZOIC STROMATOLITE

A mound of algal threads bonded with sand and mud (*Collenia* sp.)

Lines of algal threads

Limestone matrix

MICROGRAPHS OF PROKARYOTES

Layered cytoplasm

Thickest part of cytoplasm

Layered cytoplasm

Thickest part of cytoplasm

FOSSIL OF A PROTEROZOIC CYANOBACTERIUM

GROUP OF LIVING CYANOBACTERIA

The Paleozoic era

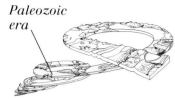

Paleozoic era

OVERVIEW OF PREHISTORIC TIMESCALE

THE PALEOZOIC ERA (550–248 million years ago) was the first era in which plant and animal life flourished. At the beginning of the Cambrian period (550–505 million years ago), a sudden burst of evolution took place: a wealth of sponges, worms, arthropods, and mollusks arose within a relatively short time. Around 100 million years later, toward the close of the Ordovician period (505–438 million years ago), the first undoubted vertebrates evolved—the jawless fishes. In the Silurian period (438–408 million years ago), arthropods and primitive plants colonized dry land. The first forests appeared in the Devonian (408–360 million years ago). The first tetrapods (four-legged vertebrates) arose from lobe-finned fishes, and gave rise to amphibians. In the Carboniferous period (360–286 million years ago), the amphibians in turn gave rise to the reptiles, and the first winged insects appeared. Throughout the Paleozoic era, the positions of the landmasses were changing and, during the Permian period (286–248 million years ago), they were brought together to form the supercontinent Pangaea. These geographical changes had profound effects on world climate, and in the Late Permian, widespread desertification across Pangaea is believed to have been the cause of the mass extinction event that brought the Paleozoic to a close.

Uncoiled final whorl

Living chamber

Umbilicus

Venter

SHELL OF AN ORDOVICIAN NAUTILOID MOLLUSK (Estonioceras sp.)

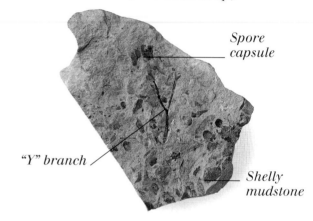

Spore capsule

"Y" branch

Shelly mudstone

LATE SILURIAN LAND PLANT (Cooksonia hemisphaerica)

KEY EVENTS IN THE PALEOZOIC ERA

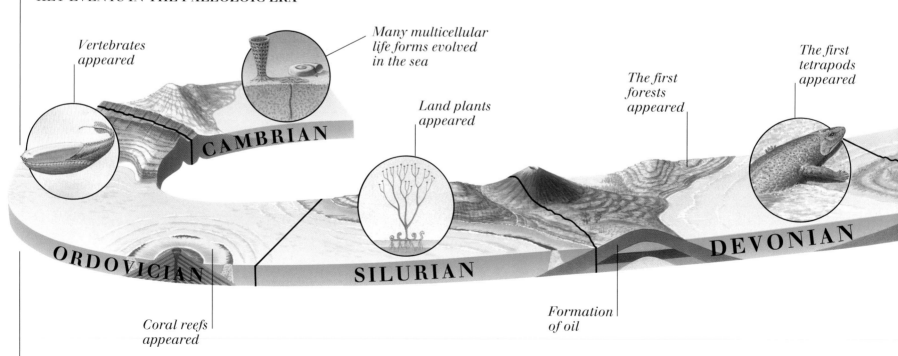

Vertebrates appeared

Many multicellular life forms evolved in the sea

Land plants appeared

The first forests appeared

The first tetrapods appeared

CAMBRIAN

ORDOVICIAN

SILURIAN

DEVONIAN

Coral reefs appeared

Formation of oil

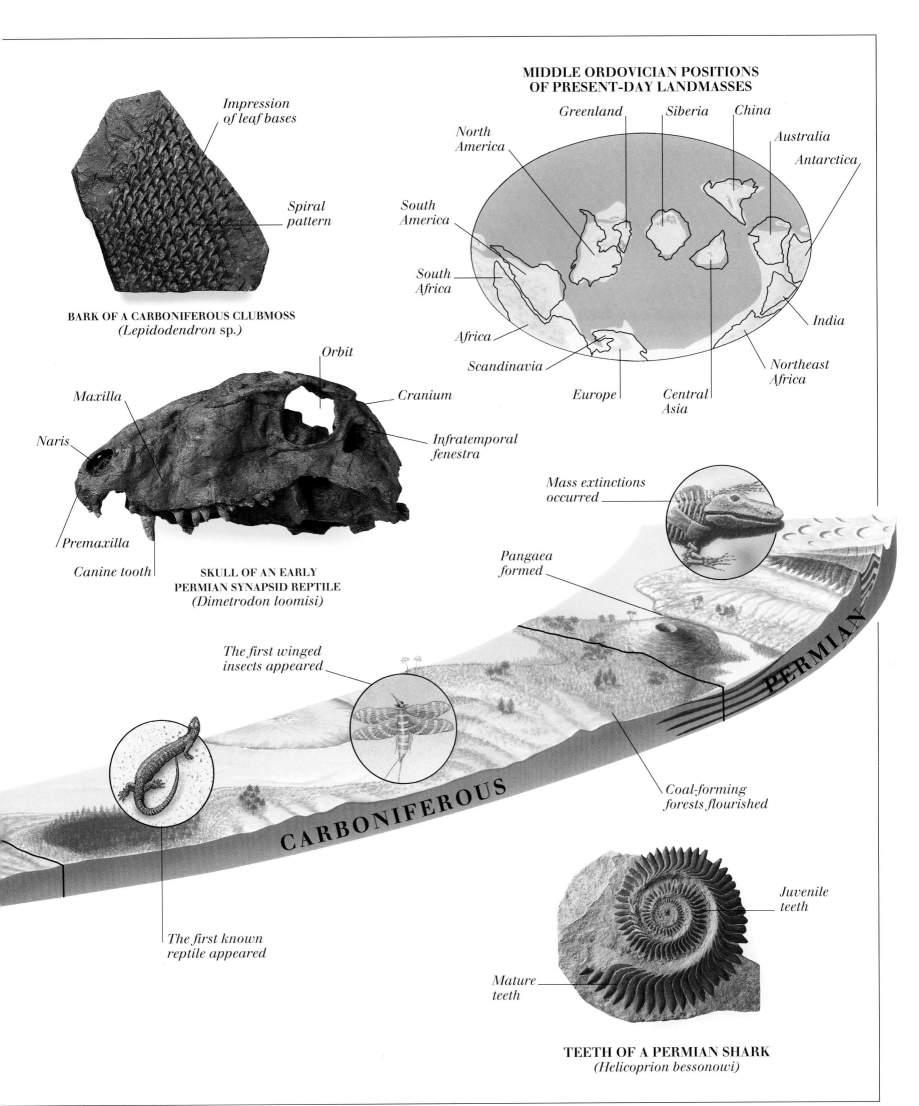

Impression of leaf bases

Spiral pattern

BARK OF A CARBONIFEROUS CLUBMOSS
(*Lepidodendron* sp.)

**MIDDLE ORDOVICIAN POSITIONS
OF PRESENT-DAY LANDMASSES**

Greenland

Siberia

China

Australia

North
America

Antarctica

South
America

South
Africa

India

Africa

Northeast
Africa

Scandinavia

Europe

Central
Asia

Maxilla

Orbit

Naris

Cranium

Infratemporal
fenestra

Premaxilla

Canine tooth

**SKULL OF AN EARLY
PERMIAN SYNAPSID REPTILE**
(*Dimetrodon loomisi*)

Mass extinctions
occurred

Pangaea
formed

The first winged
insects appeared

Coal-forming
forests flourished

PERMIAN

CARBONIFEROUS

The first known
reptile appeared

Juvenile
teeth

Mature
teeth

TEETH OF A PERMIAN SHARK
(*Helicoprion bessonowi*)

The Mesozoic era

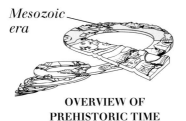

Mesozoic era

OVERVIEW OF PREHISTORIC TIME

THE MESOZOIC ERA (248–65 MILLION years ago) began with the landmasses still joined together as the supercontinent Pangaea. Warm or mild climates favored the spread of the cold-blooded reptiles, and during the Triassic period (248–208 million years ago) a number of pioneering reptile groups evolved and became extinct. Longer-lasting groups, such as turtles, crocodilians, pterosaurs, ichthyosaurs, and dinosaurs, appeared in the Late Triassic. Mammals, too, arose in this time, but remained small for over 140 million years, their development restrained by predation and competition from reptiles. In the Jurassic period (208–144 million years ago), geological movements caused Pangaea to split up into the beginnings of today's continents. Flowering plants became widespread during the Cretaceous period (144–65 million years ago). The end of the Mesozoic era was marked by the mass extinction of dinosaurs, pterosaurs, the large sea reptiles, and many other animals. An explanation is suggested by the immense crater of an asteroid that fell in Mexico 65 million years ago. Dust from the explosion may have caused a worldwide winter, unsurvivable for almost all large animals.

Pinnate leaf

Pinna (leaflet)

Rachis (main axis of leaf)

Trunk covered by leaf scales

A MODERN CYCAD
(Cycas revoluta)

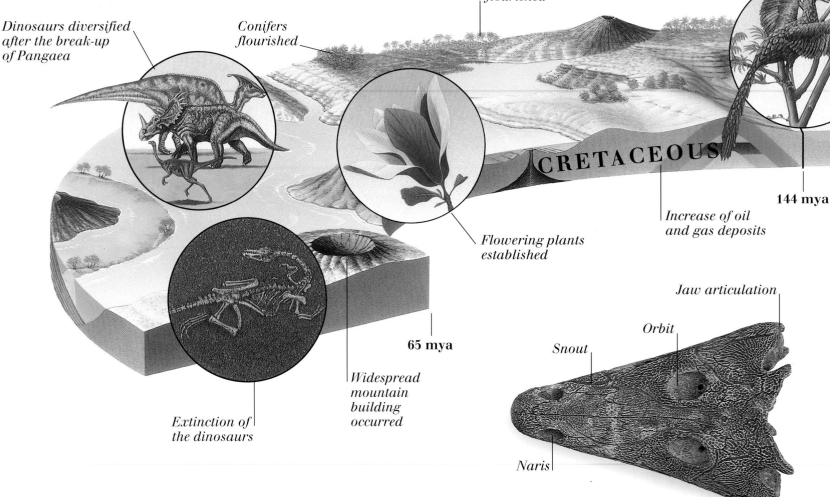

Dinosaurs diversified after the break-up of Pangaea

Conifers flourished

Cycads flourished

Birds appeared

CRETACEOUS

144 mya

Increase of oil and gas deposits

Flowering plants established

65 mya

Extinction of the dinosaurs

Widespread mountain building occurred

Jaw articulation

Orbit

Snout

Naris

A TRIASSIC AMPHIBIAN
(Benthosuchus sp.)

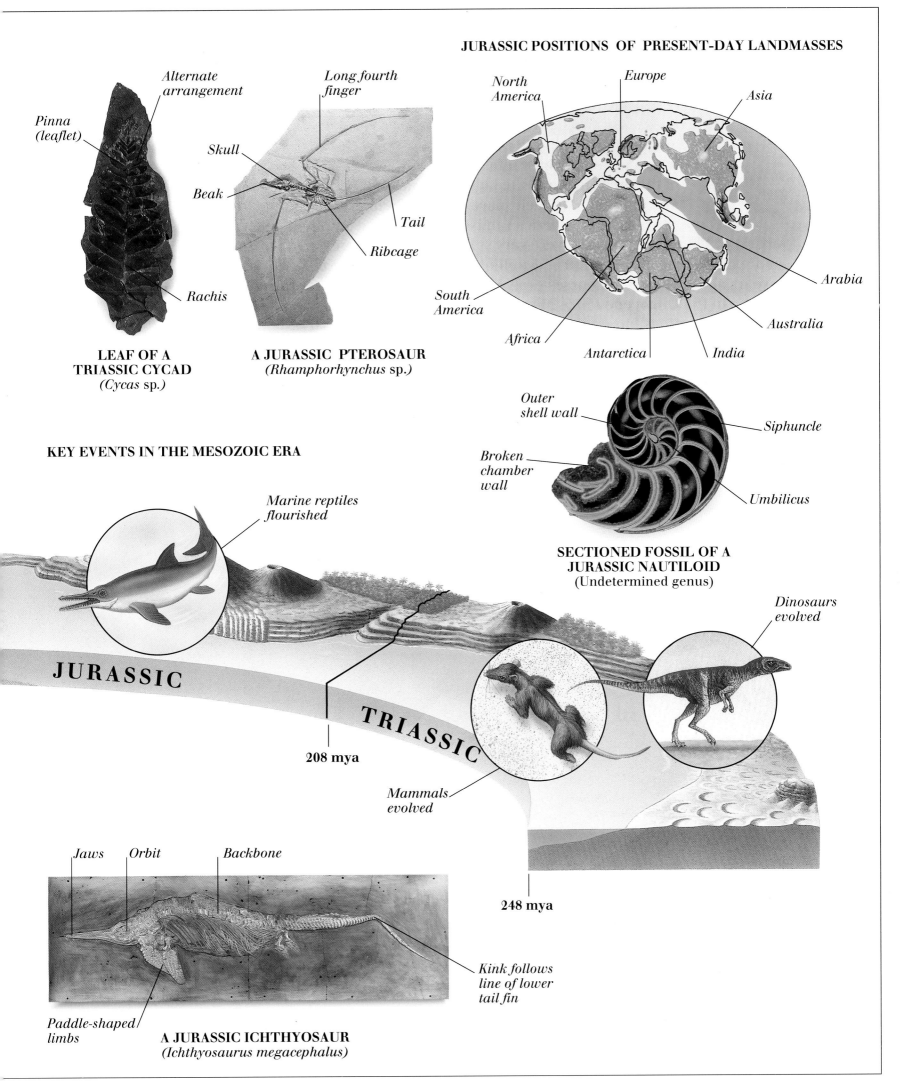

Pinna
(leaflet)

Alternate
arrangement

Long fourth
finger

Skull

Beak

Tail

Ribcage

Rachis

**LEAF OF A
TRIASSIC CYCAD**
(*Cycas* sp.)

A JURASSIC PTEROSAUR
(*Rhamphorhynchus* sp.)

JURASSIC POSITIONS OF PRESENT-DAY LANDMASSES

North
America

Europe

Asia

South
America

Arabia

Africa

Australia

Antarctica

India

Outer
shell wall

Siphuncle

Broken
chamber
wall

Umbilicus

**SECTIONED FOSSIL OF A
JURASSIC NAUTILOID**
(Undetermined genus)

KEY EVENTS IN THE MESOZOIC ERA

Marine reptiles
flourished

Dinosaurs
evolved

JURASSIC

TRIASSIC

208 mya

Mammals
evolved

248 mya

Jaws

Orbit

Backbone

Kink follows
line of lower
tail fin

Paddle-shaped
limbs

A JURASSIC ICHTHYOSAUR
(*Ichthyosaurus megacephalus*)

The Cenozoic era

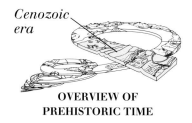

Cenozoic era

OVERVIEW OF PREHISTORIC TIME

THE CENOZOIC ERA COVERS THE LAST 65 million years, and consists of two periods, the Tertiary (65–2 million years ago), and the Quaternary (2 million years ago–present), both of which are subdivided into epochs. Following the extinction of the dinosaurs and the large sea reptiles, mammals spread and multiplied in their place, among them groups unique to the newly isolated continents of South America (an island from 73 to 3 million years ago), and Australia. The first mammals were very small, and none larger than a rat appeared before the Paleocene epoch (65–53 million years ago). In the Eocene (53–36.5 million years ago), whales and horses evolved, although the first horse was no bigger than a fox. In the Oligocene (36.5–23 million years ago), grasslands appeared, presenting new opportunities for grazing mammals and their predators. Grasslands continued their advance through the Miocene (23–5.3 million years ago) and the Pliocene (5.3–2 million years ago). The first epoch of the Quaternary period was the Pleistocene (2 million–10,000 years ago), in which a series of icy phases gripped the Northern Hemisphere. The Holocene, the epoch in which we now live, is no more than a temporary warm spell preceding the next icy phase.

SHELL OF A PLIOCENE MOLLUSK
(*Ecphora quadricostata*)

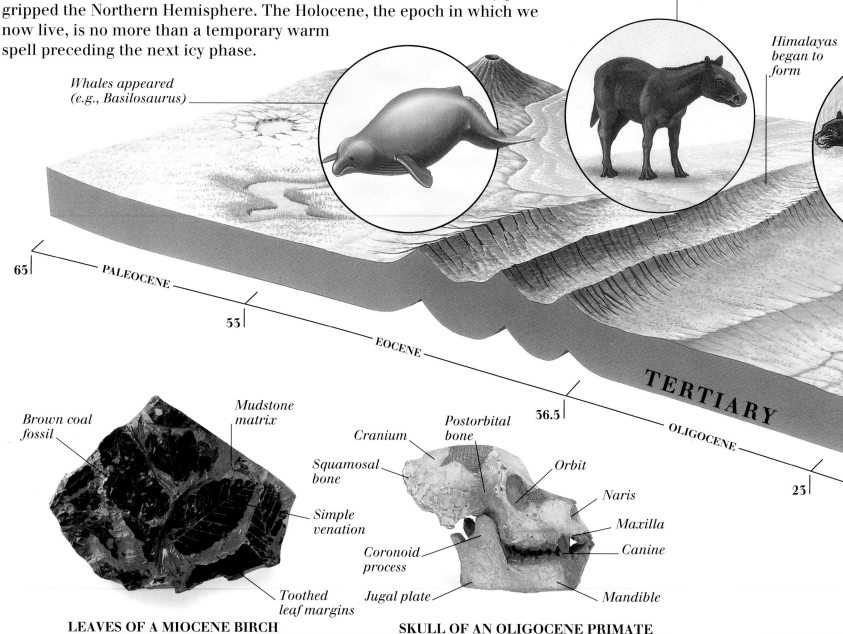

Whales appeared (e.g., Basilosaurus)

Horses appeared (e.g., Hyracotherium)

Himalayas began to form

65

PALEOCENE

53

EOCENE

36.5

OLIGOCENE

23

TERTIARY

Brown coal fossil

Mudstone matrix

Simple venation

Toothed leaf margins

LEAVES OF A MIOCENE BIRCH
(*Betula sp.*)

Cranium

Squamosal bone

Postorbital bone

Orbit

Naris

Maxilla

Canine

Coronoid process

Jugal plate

Mandible

SKULL OF AN OLIGOCENE PRIMATE
(*Aegyptopithecus sp.*)

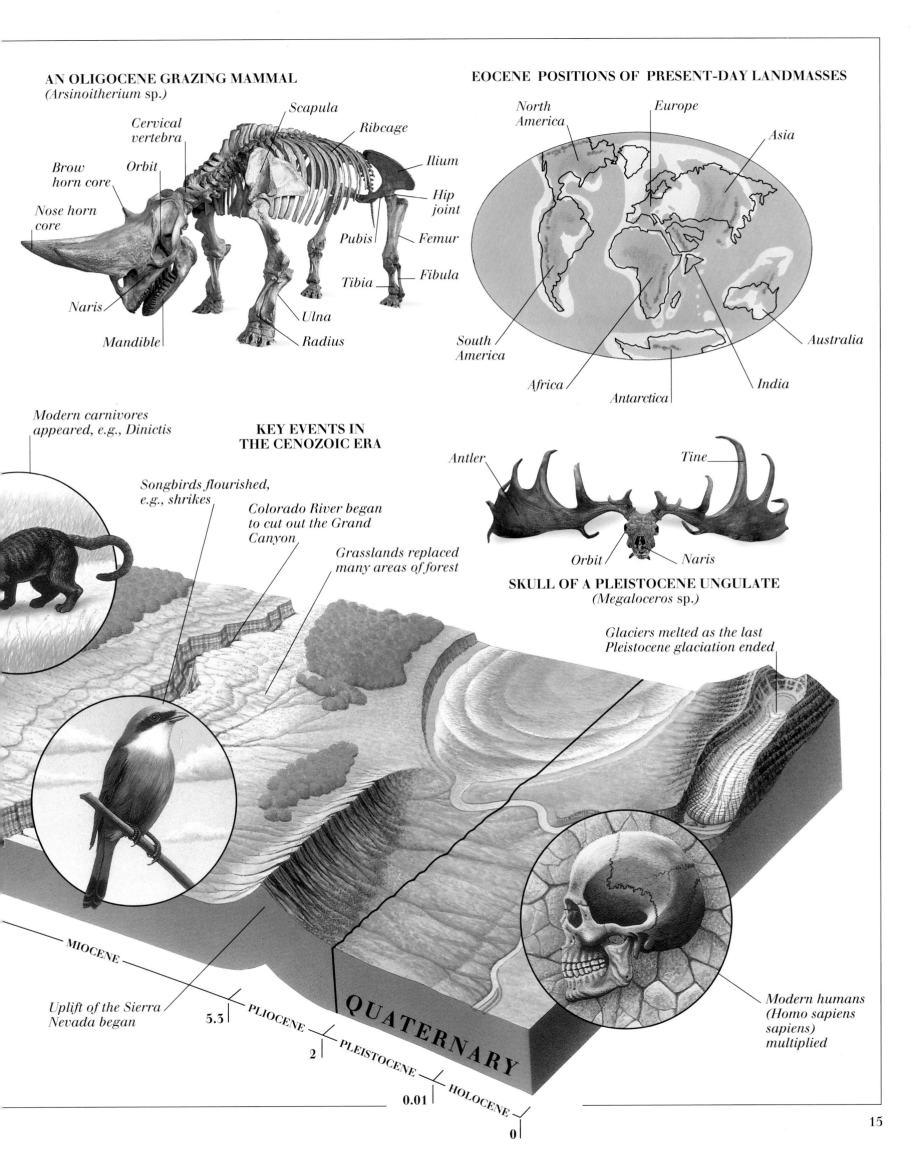

AN OLIGOCENE GRAZING MAMMAL
(Arsinoitherium sp.)

Cervical vertebra

Scapula

Ribcage

Brow horn core

Orbit

Ilium

Nose horn core

Hip joint

Pubis

Femur

Naris

Tibia

Fibula

Mandible

Ulna

Radius

EOCENE POSITIONS OF PRESENT-DAY LANDMASSES

North America

Europe

Asia

South America

Africa

Antarctica

India

Australia

Modern carnivores appeared, e.g., Dinictis

KEY EVENTS IN THE CENOZOIC ERA

Antler

Tine

Songbirds flourished, e.g., shrikes

Colorado River began to cut out the Grand Canyon

Grasslands replaced many areas of forest

Orbit

Naris

SKULL OF A PLEISTOCENE UNGULATE
(Megaloceros sp.)

Glaciers melted as the last Pleistocene glaciation ended

MIOCENE

Uplift of the Sierra Nevada began

5.3

PLIOCENE

2

PLEISTOCENE

QUATERNARY

Modern humans (Homo sapiens sapiens) multiplied

0.01

HOLOCENE

0

15

Spore-bearing plants

ALGAE GAVE RISE TO THE FIRST spore plants during
the Silurian period (438–408 million years ago).
Most land plants other than mosses and
liverworts are vascular plants: that is,
they contain tubes that carry sap, and their
stems contain especially tough cells that enable
them to stand upright on dry land. The earliest
known vascular plant is *Cooksonia* (see p. 10),
from 422 million years ago. In the next 30 million
years, many new forms of land plants evolved,
including the Devonian *Aglaophyton*. Horsetails,
ferns, and clubmosses appeared in the Devonian
period (408–360 million years ago), and are known
collectively as pteridophytes. The pteridophytes gradually
increased in size, the largest clubmosses and horsetails
growing in the coal-forming swamps of the Late Carboniferous (320–286
million years ago). All spore-bearing plants reproduce in alternate
generations. Plants of one generation (sporophytes) produce spores,
which grow into the gametophyte generation, in which male and
female sex cells (gametes) appear. The male fertilizes the female,
giving rise to a new generation of sporophytes. In heterosporous forms,
such as the clubmoss *Selaginella*, the sporophyte produces spores of two
types. The male spore (microspore) and the female spore (megaspore) give
rise to separate gametophytes. Fertilization then leads to the growth of
a new sporophyte.

AGLAOPHYTON

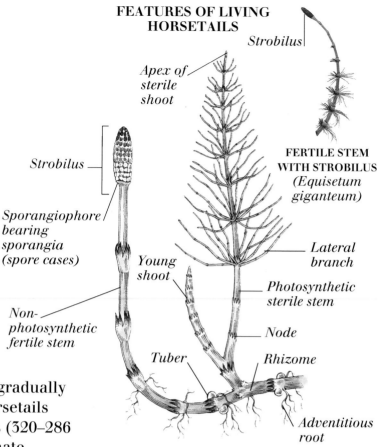

FEATURES OF LIVING HORSETAILS

Strobilus

Apex of sterile shoot

Strobilus

Sporangiophore bearing sporangia (spore cases)

Young shoot

Non-photosynthetic fertile stem

Tuber

FERTILE STEM WITH STROBILUS
(*Equisetum giganteum*)

Lateral branch

Photosynthetic sterile stem

Node

Rhizome

Adventitious root

MAIN STRUCTURES

Spore

Elater

SPORE
(*Equisetum* sp.)

FOSSILS OF EARLY PLANTS

Outline of whole plant

BYTHOTREPHIS

Impression fossil

Simple branching structure

LATE SILURIAN BROWN ALGA
(*Bythotrephis gracilis*)

Thallus

HEXAGONOCAULON

Simple branching structure

Carbonaceous film (remains of plant)

MESOZOIC THALLOID LIVERWORT
(*Hexagonocaulon minutum*)

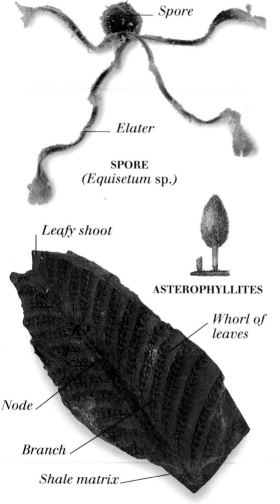

Leafy shoot

ASTEROPHYLLITES

Whorl of leaves

Node

Branch

Shale matrix

LATE CARBONIFEROUS GIANT HORSETAIL
(*Asterophyllites equisetiformis*)

MICROGRAPHS OF FOSSIL AND LIVING FERN SPORES

SPORE OF A TERTIARY FERN
(*Cyatheacidites annulata*)

SPORE OF A MESOZOIC FERN
(*Matonia braunii*)

SPORE OF A LIVING FERN
(*Matonia pectinata*)

SPORE OF A LIVING FERN
(*Matonia pectinata*
var. *foxworthyi*)

*Perispore
(outer coat)*

SPORANGIA OF A LIVING FERN
(*Pronephrium asperum*)

FEATURES OF A CARBONIFEROUS GIANT CLUBMOSS (*Lepidodendron* sp.)

Branch

Leaves

Cone

*Swollen
bases of
leaves*

*Cortex
(rigid tissue
supporting
the tree)*

*Swollen
leaf base*

*Trunk, up to
39 ft (12 m) tall*

*Vascular
tissue*

**SECTION OF STEM
SHOWING VASCULAR
STRUCTURE**

*Short,
fine root*

*Rhizophore
(root-bearing structure)*

STRUCTURE OF WHOLE TREE

*Concretion
of clay and
ironstone*

*Three-
dimensional
fossil*

FOSSIL CONE
(placed in genus *Lepidostrobus*)

LIFE CYCLE OF A HETEROSPOROUS CLUBMOSS (*Selaginella* sp.)

Microsporangium

Sporophyll

Microsporangium

Sporophyll

Megasporangium

**CONE DEVELOPS
SPORANGIA**

Microsporangium

Sporophyll

*Microspore
(male
spore)*

**RELEASE OF
MICROSPORES**

*Megaspore
(female
spore)*

Sporophyll

Megasporangium

**RELEASE OF
MEGASPORES**

*Male gamete
escaping*

*Male
gametophyte*

MICROSPORE OPENS

*Male gamete
enters archegonium
(female sex organ)*

*Female
gametophyte*

*Wall of
megaspore*

FERTILIZATION

Embryo

**EMBRYO
DEVELOPS**

Sporophyte

*Female
gametophyte*

*Remains of
megaspore*

**NEW SPOROPHYTE
DEVELOPS**

Gymnosperms

GYMNOSPERMS ARE PLANTS THAT BEAR SEEDS but not flowers. In a typical gymnosperm life cycle, pollen drifts in the air to the ovule, where it releases the male gamete (sperm), which fertilizes the egg. There is much variety in the way in which the male gamete reaches the egg; in cycads, a short pollen tube foreshadows the long pollen tubes of conifers and flowering plants (see p. 21). The cycad male gamete is motile (able to swim) and thus can complete its journey. The earliest gymnosperms were seed ferns, which appeared in the Devonian period (408–360 million years ago) and died out in the Mesozoic era (see pp. 12–13). Cycads arose in the Permian (286–248 million years ago), and some species survive in scattered tropical and warm-temperate regions of the world. The maidenhair trees (ginkgos) had a worldwide distribution in the Mesozoic, but the single surviving species grows (as a wild plant) only in a small part of China. Conifers have the longest fossil record of all gymnosperms, their earliest record coming from the Late Carboniferous (320–286 million years ago). The conifers began to diversify in the Permian, and continued in the Mesozoic. Even though the flowering plants forced them out of many habitats, conifers still dominate large areas of the world's vegetation today.

SEEDS OF A CARBONIFEROUS SEED FERN (*Trigonocarpus adamsi*)

Rib on seed surface

TRIGONOCARPUS

Striated surface

SECTIONS THROUGH LIVING PINE CONES (*Pinus silvestris*)

Microsporophyll (modified leaf that carries microsporangia)

Microsporangium (structure in which pollen grains are formed)

Ovuliferous scale (ovule-bearing structure)

Bract scale

Ovule (structure containing female gametes)

Axis of cone

Scale leaf

SECOND-YEAR FEMALE CONE

YOUNG MALE CONE

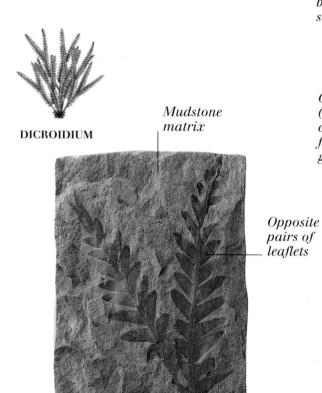

DICROIDIUM

Mudstone matrix

Opposite pairs of leaflets

"Y"-forked leaf

FOSSIL OF A TRIASSIC SEED FERN
(*Dicroidium* sp.)

MICROGRAPHS OF POLLEN GRAINS OF LIVING GYMNOSPERMS

Papilla

Exine (outer coat of pollen grain)

MAIDENHAIR TREE
(*Ginkgo biloba*)

JAPANESE CEDAR
(*Cryptomeria japonica*)

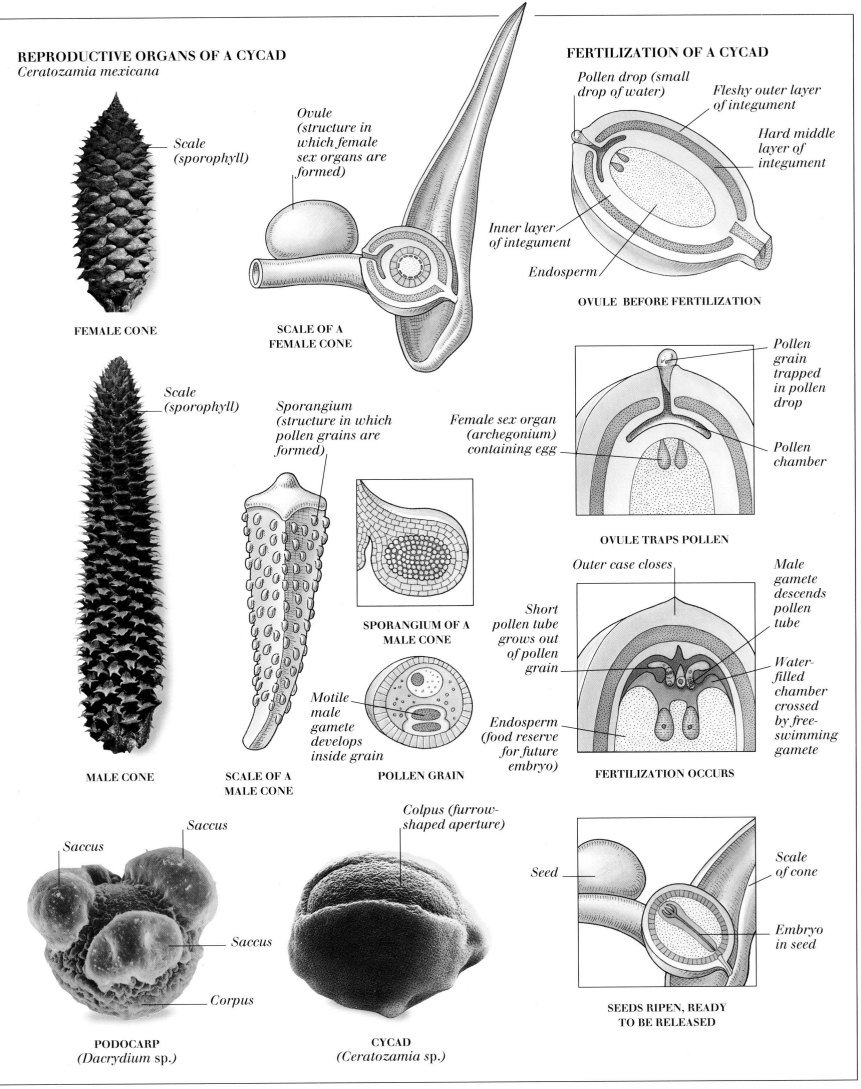

REPRODUCTIVE ORGANS OF A CYCAD
Ceratozamia mexicana

Scale
(sporophyll)

FEMALE CONE

*Ovule
(structure in
which female
sex organs are
formed)*

**SCALE OF A
FEMALE CONE**

Scale
(sporophyll)

*Sporangium
(structure in which
pollen grains are
formed)*

MALE CONE

**SCALE OF A
MALE CONE**

**SPORANGIUM OF A
MALE CONE**

*Motile
male
gamete
develops
inside grain*

POLLEN GRAIN

Saccus

Saccus

Saccus

Corpus

PODOCARP
(*Dacrydium* sp.)

*Colpus (furrow-
shaped aperture)*

CYCAD
(*Ceratozamia* sp.)

FERTILIZATION OF A CYCAD

*Pollen drop (small
drop of water)*

*Fleshy outer layer
of integument*

*Hard middle
layer of
integument*

*Inner layer
of integument*

Endosperm

OVULE BEFORE FERTILIZATION

*Pollen
grain
trapped
in pollen
drop*

*Female sex organ
(archegonium)
containing egg*

*Pollen
chamber*

OVULE TRAPS POLLEN

Outer case closes

*Male
gamete
descends
pollen
tube*

*Short
pollen tube
grows out
of pollen
grain*

*Endosperm
(food reserve
for future
embryo)*

*Water-
filled
chamber
crossed
by free-
swimming
gamete*

FERTILIZATION OCCURS

Seed

*Scale
of cone*

*Embryo
in seed*

**SEEDS RIPEN, READY
TO BE RELEASED**

Flowering plants

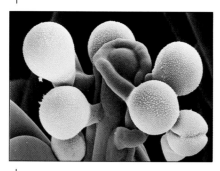

GERMINATING POLLEN OF A POPPY

FLOWERING PLANTS (ANGIOSPERMS) diversified rapidly in the middle of the Cretaceous, some 100 million years ago, to become the dominant group in the world's flora. Flowers are difficult to categorize, but there are two features common to nearly all angiosperms: the ovule (seed) is enclosed within an ovary (fruit), and there is a double fertilization process. Two male gamete nuclei are brought by the pollen tube into the same ovule, one fertilizing the egg and the other the surrounding material which becomes a food supply for the seed. The earliest angiosperm families were perhaps related to modern laurels and magnolias, but with flowers that were smaller and simpler. Soon after the great diversification had begun, perhaps 95 million years ago, relatives of the modern hazelnuts, roses, and lilies already existed. The split of the angiosperms into dicotyledons (with two seed leaves) and monocotyledons (with one) had happened during the Early Cretaceous. Dicotyledons are the larger group (with 250 living families), and include all the fossil flowers and pollen grains shown here. Monocotyledons (with 50 living families) include palms, bulb plants, and grasses. Grasses spread throughout the world in the Tertiary period (65–2 million years ago), and by the Miocene epoch (23–5.3 million years ago) grassland was one of the world's great ecosystems.

RECONSTRUCTION OF A LATE CRETACEOUS FLOWER
(Silvianthemum suecicum)

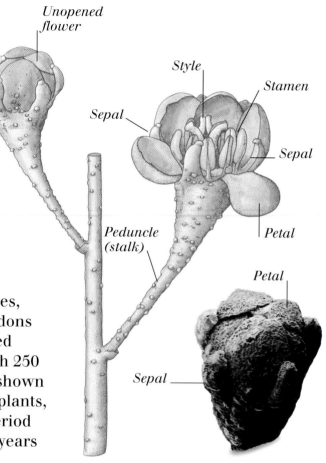

Unopened flower

Style

Stamen

Sepal

Sepal

Petal

Peduncle (stalk)

Petal

Sepal

FOSSIL OF UNOPENED FLOWER
80 million years old

MICROGRAPHS OF FOSSIL FLOWERS FROM THE CRETACEOUS

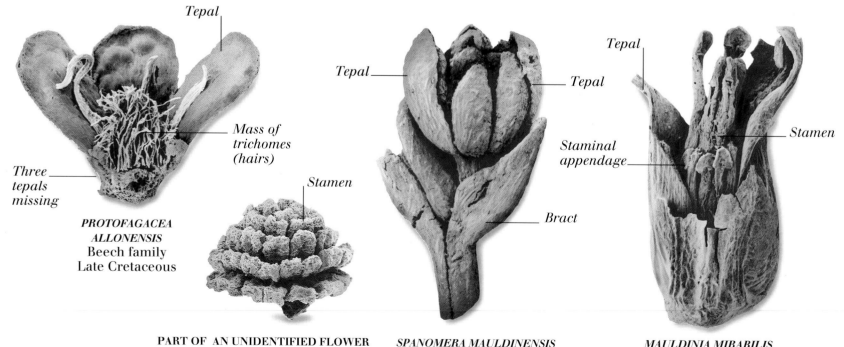

Tepal

Mass of trichomes (hairs)

Three tepals missing

PROTOFAGACEA ALLONENSIS
Beech family
Late Cretaceous

Stamen

PART OF AN UNIDENTIFIED FLOWER
Oldest known fossil of a floral structure
Early Cretaceous (120 million years old)

Tepal

Tepal

Bract

SPANOMERA MAULDINENSIS
Related to boxwood family
Middle Cretaceous

Tepal

Staminal appendage

Stamen

MAULDINIA MIRABILIS
Laurel family
Late Cretaceous

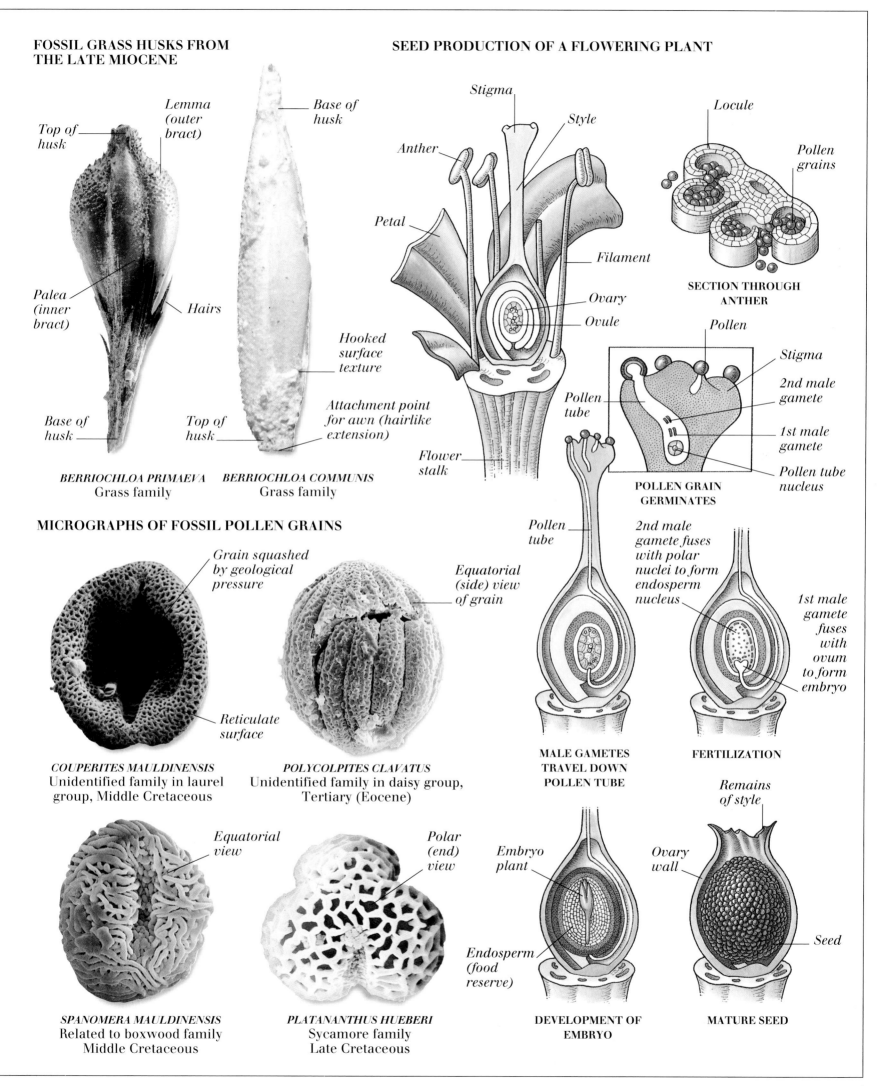

FOSSIL GRASS HUSKS FROM THE LATE MIOCENE

Top of husk

Lemma (outer bract)

Palea (inner bract)

Hairs

Base of husk

Base of husk

Top of husk

Hooked surface texture

Attachment point for awn (hairlike extension)

BERRIOCHLOA PRIMAEVA
Grass family

BERRIOCHLOA COMMUNIS
Grass family

MICROGRAPHS OF FOSSIL POLLEN GRAINS

Grain squashed by geological pressure

Reticulate surface

Equatorial (side) view of grain

COUPERITES MAULDINENSIS
Unidentified family in laurel group, Middle Cretaceous

POLYCOLPITES CLAVATUS
Unidentified family in daisy group, Tertiary (Eocene)

Equatorial view

Polar (end) view

SPANOMERA MAULDINENSIS
Related to boxwood family
Middle Cretaceous

PLATANANTHUS HUEBERI
Sycamore family
Late Cretaceous

SEED PRODUCTION OF A FLOWERING PLANT

Stigma

Style

Anther

Petal

Filament

Ovary

Ovule

Flower stalk

Locule

Pollen grains

SECTION THROUGH ANTHER

Pollen

Stigma

2nd male gamete

1st male gamete

Pollen tube

Pollen tube nucleus

POLLEN GRAIN GERMINATES

Pollen tube

2nd male gamete fuses with polar nuclei to form endosperm nucleus

1st male gamete fuses with ovum to form embryo

MALE GAMETES TRAVEL DOWN POLLEN TUBE

FERTILIZATION

Embryo plant

Endosperm (food reserve)

Remains of style

Ovary wall

Seed

DEVELOPMENT OF EMBRYO

MATURE SEED

Early invertebrates

THE GREAT EVOLUTIONARY EXPLOSION of the Cambrian period (550–505 million years ago) saw a huge diversification of invertebrates—animals without backbones. All were sea-dwelling, and most had outer skeletons to support and guard their soft, vulnerable bodies. Among them were sponges: sedentary, aquatic animals with simple, baglike bodies made of many cells. Cnidarians, for example corals and sea anemones, were more

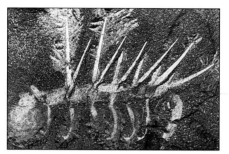

HALLUCIGENIA

advanced, with stinging tentacles to bring prey to the mouth. Graptolites were a group of wormlike colonial organisms that lived from the Cambrian to the Carboniferous (550–320 million years ago). Scientists may reclassify a related living group (the pterobranchs) as graptolites, in which case they would no longer be extinct. A graptolite colony was made of many individuals (zooids), each building a protective cup (theca). The resulting row of cups (a rhabdosome) often produced a saw-edged fossil (see p. 57). The bizarre *Hallucigenia*, a velvet worm, was one of the animals discovered in the 530-million-year-old Burgess Shale in Canada. It had seven pairs of spines and seven pairs of legs. Polychaetes, such as *Serpula* and *Rotularia*, are annelids: worms with a body made of many segments. Bryozoans are tiny animals whose colonies either lie flat or grow upward and branch like trees.

EARLY GROWTH STAGE OF A GRAPTOLITE RHABDOSOME

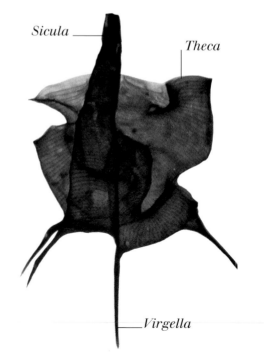

Sicula

Theca

Virgella

ORDOVICIAN GRAPTOLITE RHABDOSOME
(*Amplexograptus maxwelli*)

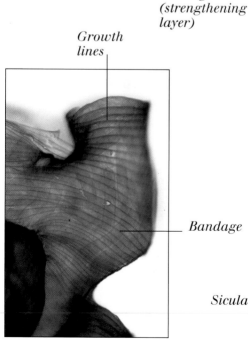

Growth lines

Bandage

ENLARGEMENT SHOWING INDIVIDUAL THECA

RECONSTRUCTION OF A GRAPTOLITE COLONY

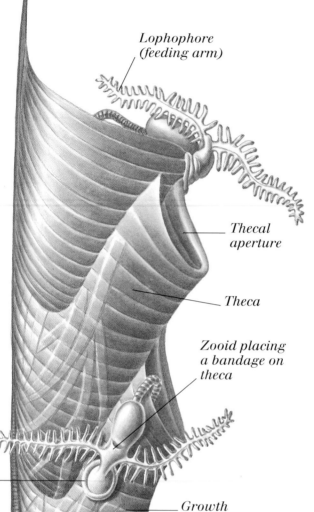

Nema

Lophophore (feeding arm)

Thecal aperture

Theca

Zooid placing a bandage on theca

Cephalic shield

Growth line

Bandage (strengthening layer)

Sicula

Virgella

Nema

Growth lines

Theca

Virgella

SILURIAN GRAPTOLITE RHABDOSOME
(*Monograptus* sp.)

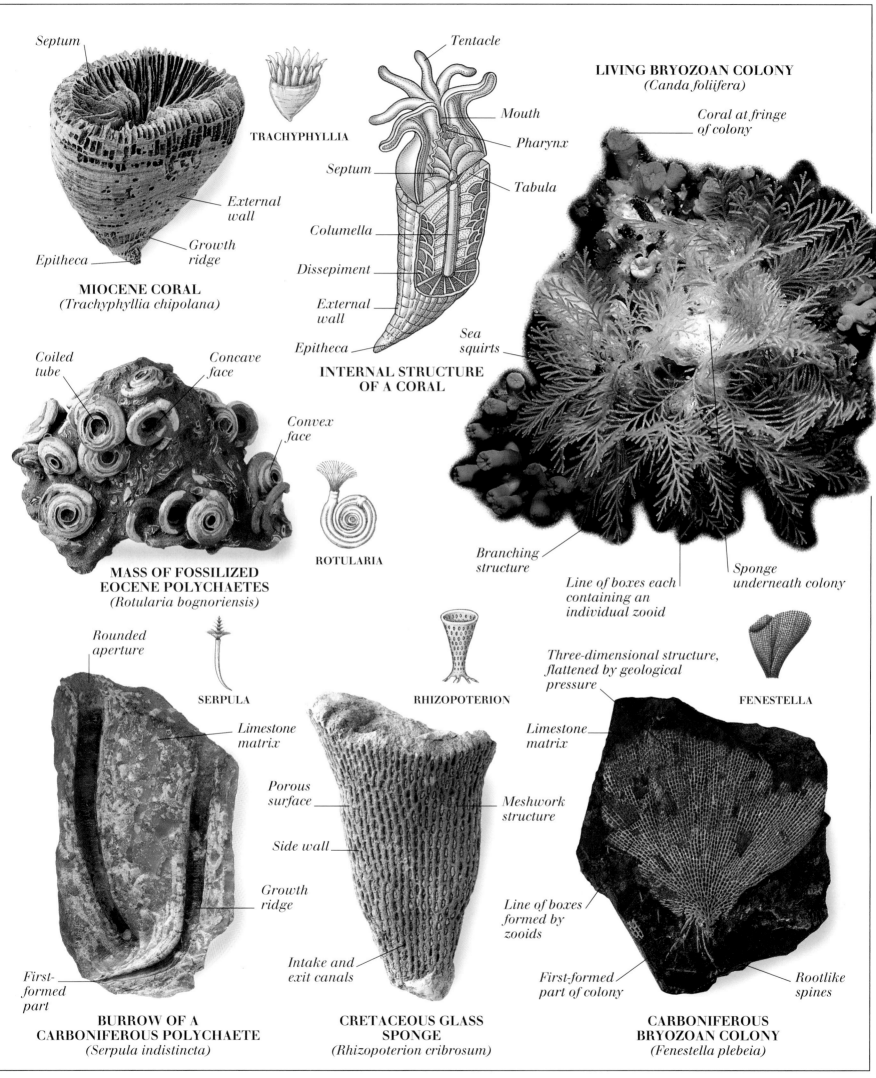

Septum

External
wall

Growth
ridge

Epitheca

MIOCENE CORAL
(Trachyphyllia chipolana)

TRACHYPHYLLIA

Tentacle

Mouth

Pharynx

Septum

Tabula

Columella

Dissepiment

External
wall

Epitheca

Sea
squirts

**INTERNAL STRUCTURE
OF A CORAL**

LIVING BRYOZOAN COLONY
(Canda foliifera)

Coral at fringe
of colony

Coiled
tube

Concave
face

Convex
face

ROTULARIA

**MASS OF FOSSILIZED
EOCENE POLYCHAETES**
(Rotularia bognoriensis)

Branching
structure

Sponge
underneath colony

Line of boxes each
containing an
individual zooid

Rounded
aperture

SERPULA

Limestone
matrix

Three-dimensional structure,
flattened by geological
pressure

FENESTELLA

Limestone
matrix

RHIZOPOTERION

Porous
surface

Meshwork
structure

Side wall

Growth
ridge

Line of boxes
formed by
zooids

First-
formed
part

Intake and
exit canals

First-formed
part of colony

Rootlike
spines

**BURROW OF A
CARBONIFEROUS POLYCHAETE**
(Serpula indistincta)

**CRETACEOUS GLASS
SPONGE**
(Rhizopoterion cribrosum)

**CARBONIFEROUS
BRYOZOAN COLONY**
(Fenestella plebeia)

Mollusks and brachiopods

BELEMNOTEUTHIS

MOLLUSKS AND BRACHIOPODS are two groups of soft-bodied marine invertebrates, most of which are shelled, that appeared in Early Cambrian times (550–530 million years ago). The three most widespread mollusk groups are: bivalves, which lack a head and have a two-part, hinged shell; gastropods, such as snails, with a distinct head and a suckerlike foot; and cephalopods. Cephalopods have a large head, tentacles, and "jet propulsion"—the ability to squirt water forward in order to swim backward. Prehistoric cephalopods included the ammonoids, the nautiloids (see p. 13), and the squidlike belemnites, which lacked external shells but had a hard internal support called a phragmocone. A fourth group of mollusks, the chitons, consists of small, sowbuglike seashore-dwellers with flattened shells made up of overlapping plates. Brachiopods were abundant in the Paleozoic, but few kinds survive today. They resemble bivalve mollusks, but their paired shell valves are not identical in size or curvature. Brachiopods live on the seabed, to which they anchor themselves with a fleshy stalk. The stalk passes through a hole in a projection known as the umbo, located at the hinge end of the larger valve.

FEATURES OF CEPHALOPODS

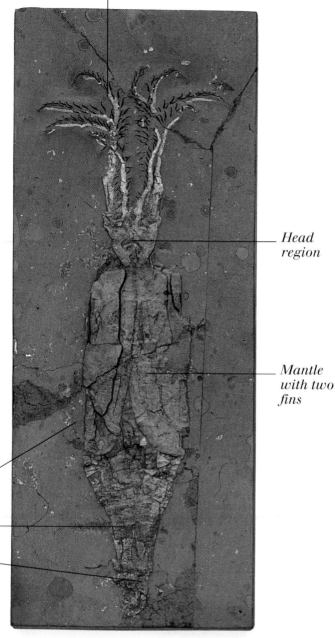

Hooked tentacle

Head region

Mantle with two fins

Shell wall

Phragmocone

Initial chamber of phragmocone

JURASSIC BELEMNITE
(*Belemnoteuthis antiqua*)

RECONSTRUCTION OF AN AMMONITE

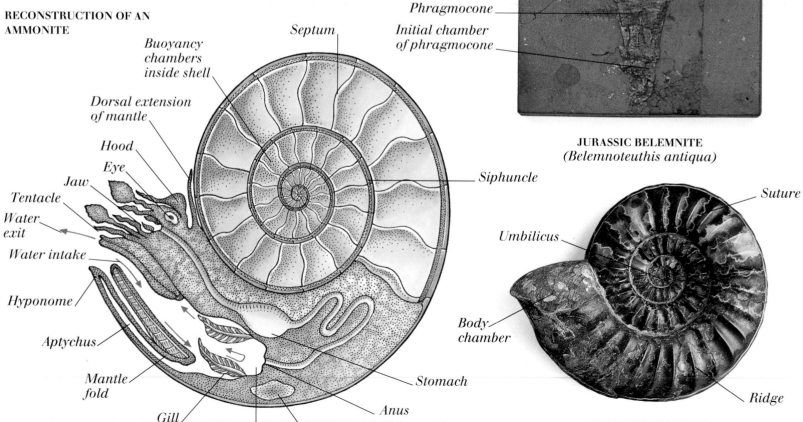

Buoyancy chambers inside shell

Septum

Dorsal extension of mantle

Hood

Eye

Jaw

Tentacle

Water exit

Water intake

Hyponome

Aptychus

Mantle fold

Gill

Branchial mantle cavity

Reproductive organ

Anus

Stomach

Siphuncle

Suture

Umbilicus

Body chamber

Ridge

JURASSIC AMMONITE SHELL
(*Asteroceras obtusum*)

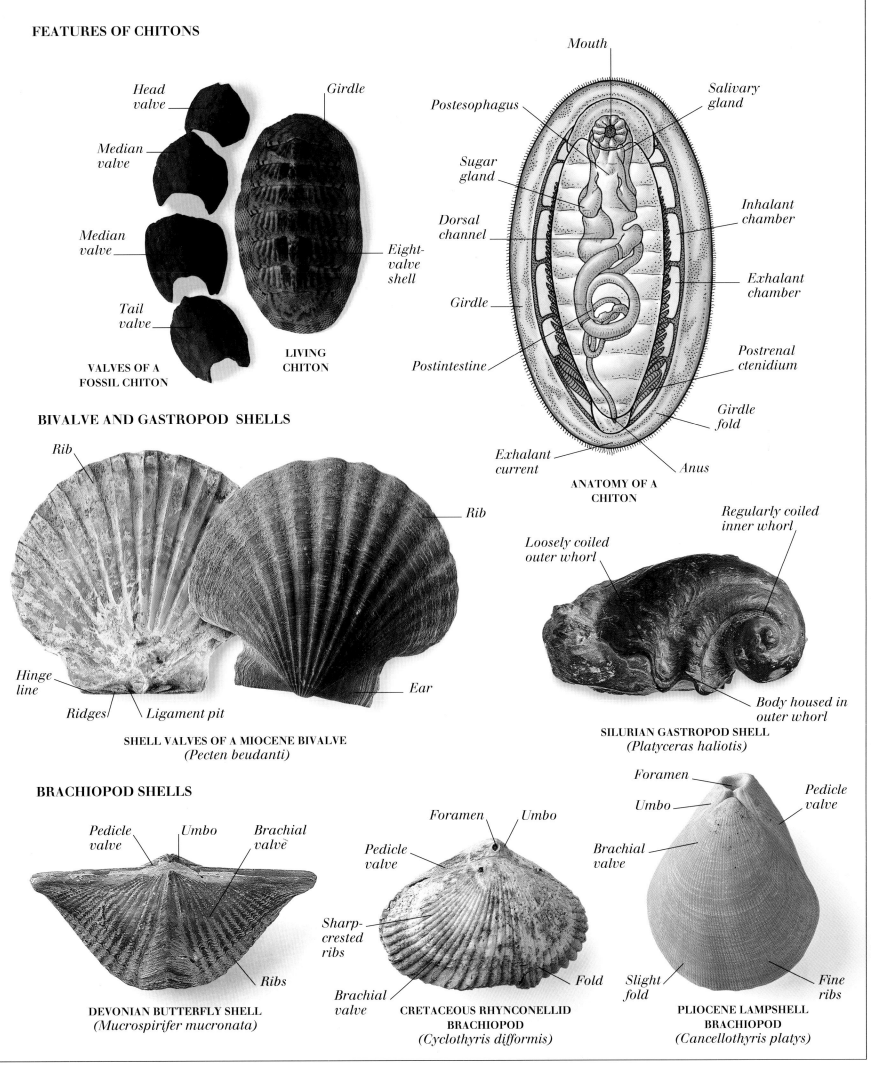

FEATURES OF CHITONS

VALVES OF A FOSSIL CHITON

Head valve

Median valve

Median valve

Tail valve

LIVING CHITON

Girdle

Eight-valve shell

ANATOMY OF A CHITON

Mouth

Postesophagus

Salivary gland

Sugar gland

Dorsal channel

Inhalant chamber

Girdle

Exhalant chamber

Postintestine

Postrenal ctenidium

Girdle fold

Exhalant current

Anus

BIVALVE AND GASTROPOD SHELLS

Rib

Rib

Hinge line

Ridges

Ligament pit

Ear

SHELL VALVES OF A MIOCENE BIVALVE
(Pecten beudanti)

Regularly coiled inner whorl

Loosely coiled outer whorl

Body housed in outer whorl

SILURIAN GASTROPOD SHELL
(Platyceras haliotis)

BRACHIOPOD SHELLS

Pedicle valve

Umbo

Brachial valve

Ribs

DEVONIAN BUTTERFLY SHELL
(Mucrospirifer mucronata)

Foramen

Umbo

Pedicle valve

Sharp-crested ribs

Brachial valve

Fold

CRETACEOUS RHYNCONELLID BRACHIOPOD
(Cyclothyris difformis)

Foramen

Pedicle valve

Umbo

Brachial valve

Slight fold

Fine ribs

PLIOCENE LAMPSHELL BRACHIOPOD
(Cancellothyris platys)

Echinoderms and arthropods

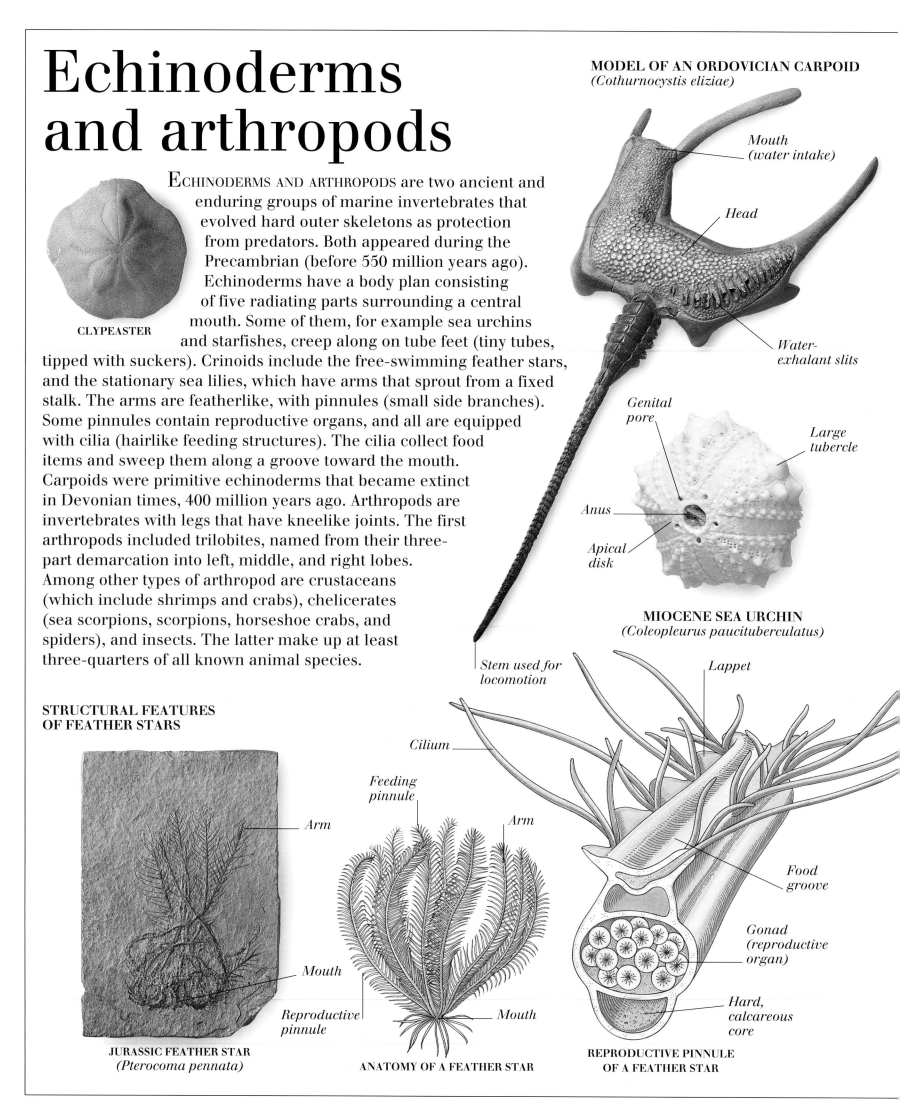

ECHINODERMS AND ARTHROPODS are two ancient and enduring groups of marine invertebrates that evolved hard outer skeletons as protection from predators. Both appeared during the Precambrian (before 550 million years ago). Echinoderms have a body plan consisting of five radiating parts surrounding a central mouth. Some of them, for example sea urchins and starfishes, creep along on tube feet (tiny tubes, tipped with suckers). Crinoids include the free-swimming feather stars, and the stationary sea lilies, which have arms that sprout from a fixed stalk. The arms are featherlike, with pinnules (small side branches). Some pinnules contain reproductive organs, and all are equipped with cilia (hairlike feeding structures). The cilia collect food items and sweep them along a groove toward the mouth. Carpoids were primitive echinoderms that became extinct in Devonian times, 400 million years ago. Arthropods are invertebrates with legs that have kneelike joints. The first arthropods included trilobites, named from their three-part demarcation into left, middle, and right lobes. Among other types of arthropod are crustaceans (which include shrimps and crabs), chelicerates (sea scorpions, scorpions, horseshoe crabs, and spiders), and insects. The latter make up at least three-quarters of all known animal species.

CLYPEASTER

MODEL OF AN ORDOVICIAN CARPOID
(*Cothurnocystis eliziae*)

Mouth
(water intake)

Head

Water-
exhalant slits

Genital
pore

Large
tubercle

Anus

Apical
disk

MIOCENE SEA URCHIN
(*Coleopleurus paucituberculatus*)

Stem used for
locomotion

Lappet

**STRUCTURAL FEATURES
OF FEATHER STARS**

Cilium

Food
groove

Arm

Feeding
pinnule

Arm

Gonad
(reproductive
organ)

Mouth

Reproductive
pinnule

Mouth

Hard,
calcareous
core

JURASSIC FEATHER STAR
(*Pterocoma pennata*)

ANATOMY OF A FEATHER STAR

**REPRODUCTIVE PINNULE
OF A FEATHER STAR**

SILURIAN SEA LILY
(Dimerocrinites icosidactylus)

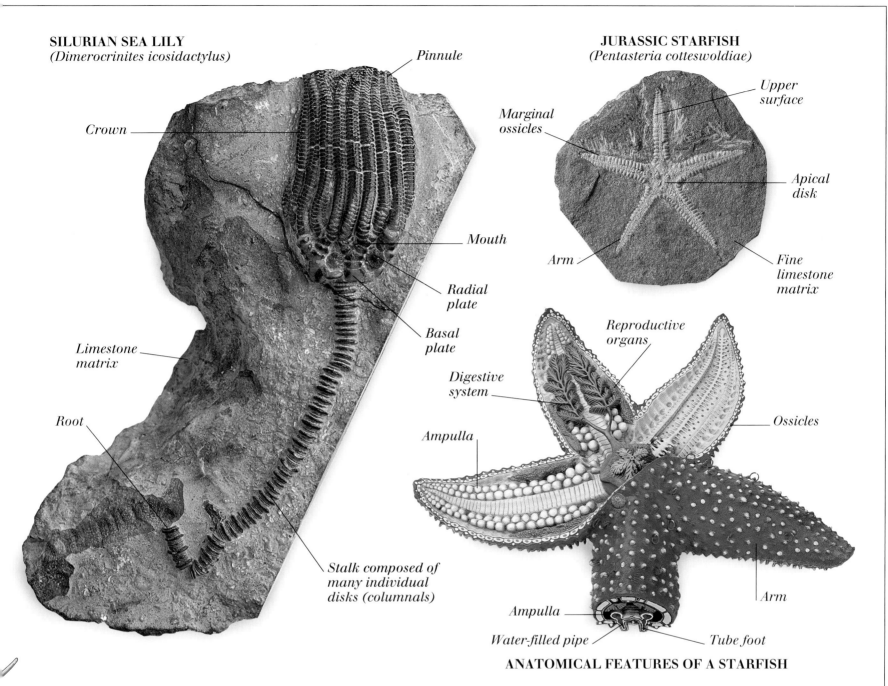

Pinnule

Crown

Mouth

Radial plate

Basal plate

Limestone matrix

Root

Stalk composed of many individual disks (columnals)

JURASSIC STARFISH
(Pentasteria cottesvoldiae)

Upper surface

Marginal ossicles

Apical disk

Arm

Fine limestone matrix

Reproductive organs

Digestive system

Ossicles

Ampulla

Arm

Ampulla

Water-filled pipe

Tube foot

ANATOMICAL FEATURES OF A STARFISH

EXAMPLES OF FOSSIL ARTHROPODS

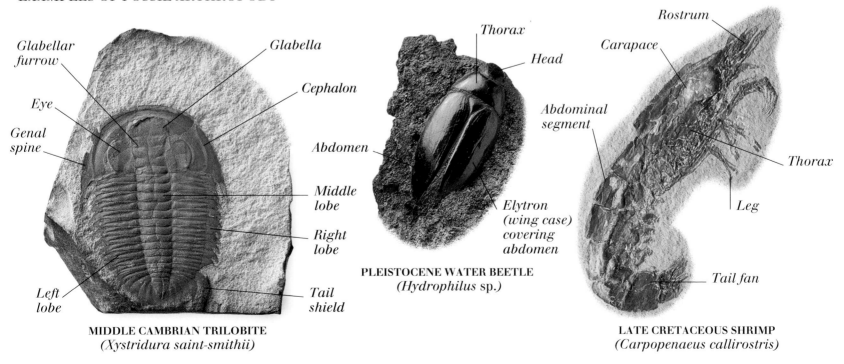

Glabellar furrow

Glabella

Eye

Cephalon

Genal spine

Middle lobe

Right lobe

Left lobe

Tail shield

MIDDLE CAMBRIAN TRILOBITE
(Xystridura saint-smithii)

Thorax

Head

Abdomen

Elytron (wing case) covering abdomen

PLEISTOCENE WATER BEETLE
(Hydrophilus sp.)

Rostrum

Carapace

Abdominal segment

Thorax

Leg

Tail fan

LATE CRETACEOUS SHRIMP
(Carpopenaeus callirostris)

Primitive fishes

THE FIRST VERTEBRATES WERE FISHES. They evolved in the Ordovician period (505–438 million years ago) from tiny marine animals called cephalochordates. These creatures still exist today and include the lancelet. The first known fishes were extremely small, lacked jaws, and had a complex brain that was protected by a skull. Their bodies were internally supported by a backbone made of bony vertebrae. Jawless fishes became extinct in the Early Carboniferous, about 340 million years ago, with the exception of a handful of species that gave rise to the modern lampreys and hagfishes. Lampreys are parasites that use their mouths to fasten onto other fishes and suck their blood. A major group among jawless fishes were the cephalaspids, the first fishes to have paired pectoral fins, an innovation that helped them keep their balance. A second class of primitive fishes, the placoderms, arose during the Devonian period. These were the first fishes with jaws (although most lacked true teeth). Placoderms had heavy bony armor that protected the head and the forepart of the body. They ranged in size from the 16-in-long (40 cm) *Bothriolepis* and the 6-in (15-cm) *Pterichthyodes* to the immense *Dunkleosteus*. This monster was 29 ft 6 in (9 m) long and had gaping jaws with jagged, toothlike edges, and was the largest predator of the Late Devonian seas.

LANCELET

EVOLVING HEAD SHIELDS OF CEPHALASPIDS

TREMATASPIS

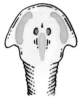

DIDYMASPIS

KIAERASPIS

THYESTES

CEPHALASPIS

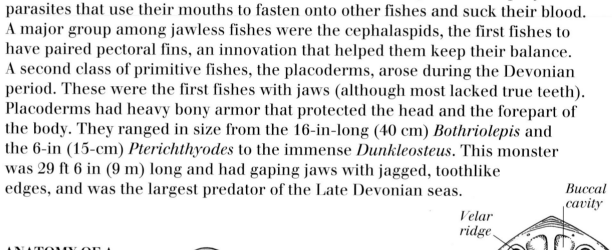

ANATOMY OF A CEPHALASPID

Mouth

Gill opening

Ventral scale

Attachment surface for pectoral fin

UNDERSIDE OF A HEAD SHIELD

Velar ridge

Spiracular gill chamber

Orbit

Esophagus

Buccal cavity

Mandibular nerve

Dorsal aorta

Vestibule

Pectoral sinus

Foramen (hole) for aorta

INTERNAL HEAD STRUCTURE

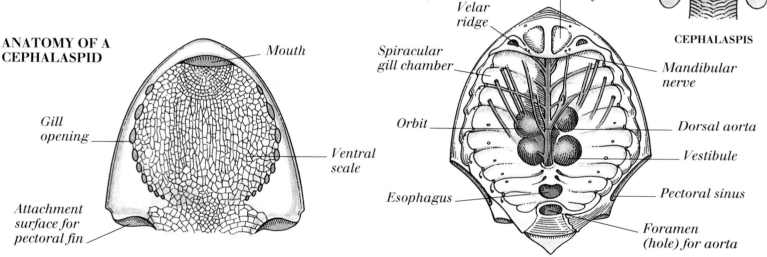

Median fin

Armor plate

Eye

Single nostril

Solid bony shield

Uptilted tail

Flat belly

Pectoral fin

Sensory panel

Position of mouth

EXTERNAL FEATURES

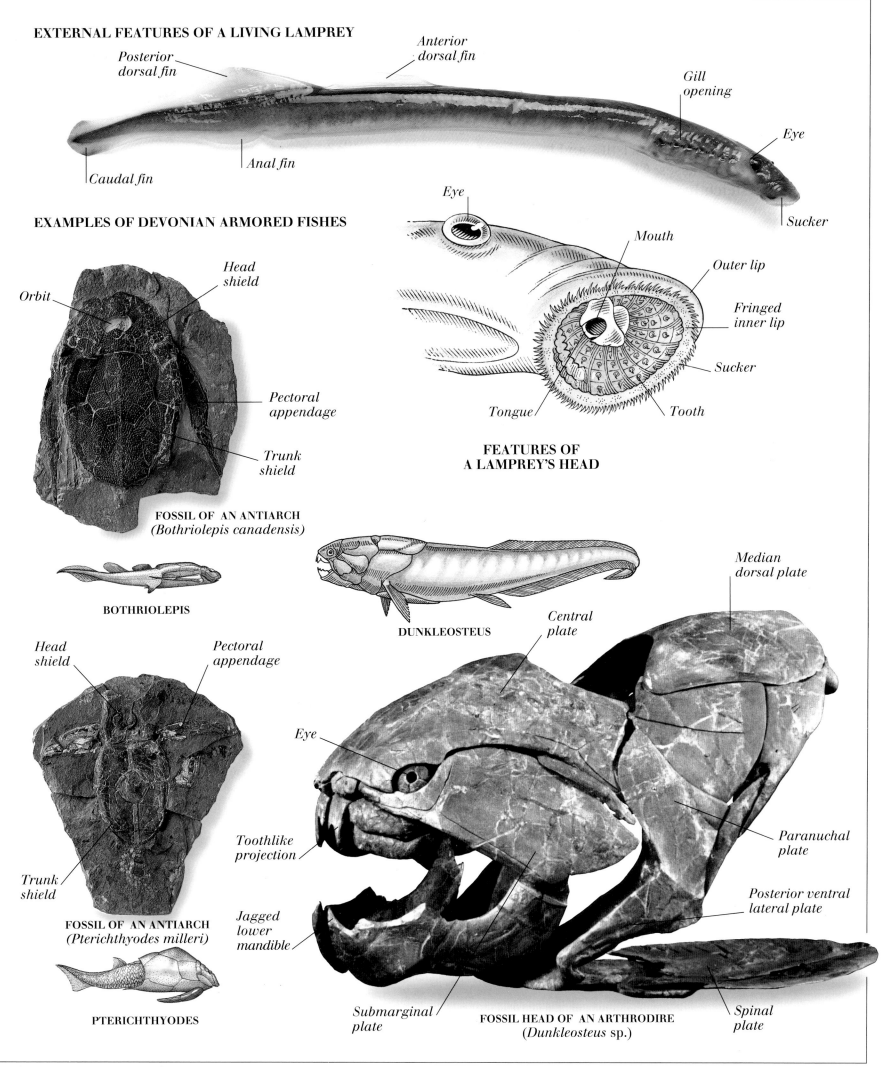

EXTERNAL FEATURES OF A LIVING LAMPREY

Posterior dorsal fin

Anterior dorsal fin

Gill opening

Eye

Anal fin

Caudal fin

Sucker

EXAMPLES OF DEVONIAN ARMORED FISHES

Eye

Mouth

Outer lip

Head shield

Orbit

Fringed inner lip

Pectoral appendage

Sucker

Trunk shield

Tongue

Tooth

**FEATURES OF
A LAMPREY'S HEAD**

FOSSIL OF AN ANTIARCH
(Bothriolepis canadensis)

BOTHRIOLEPIS

Median dorsal plate

DUNKLEOSTEUS

Central plate

Head shield

Pectoral appendage

Eye

Toothlike projection

Paranuchal plate

Trunk shield

Posterior ventral lateral plate

FOSSIL OF AN ANTIARCH
(Pterichthyodes milleri)

Jagged lower mandible

Submarginal plate

Spinal plate

PTERICHTHYODES

FOSSIL HEAD OF AN ARTHRODIRE
(Dunkleosteus sp.)

The rise of modern fishes

WITH THE EXCEPTION OF HAGFISHES and lampreys, all living fishes fall into two classes: Chondrichthyes (cartilaginous fishes), and Osteichthyes (bony fishes). Both classes evolved from a single ancestor in Late Silurian times, some 410 million years ago. They can be distinguished from the primitive fishes (see pp. 24–25) by their jaw structure and by the fact that their teeth are continually replaced throughout life. Cartilaginous fishes (sharks, rays, and their relatives) have gristly skeletons and small, toothlike scales, and they lack swim bladders. An example is the Early Eocene *Heliobatis*. Bony fishes, which include most living fishes, have bony skeletons, small, overlapping scales, and a gas-filled swim bladder, used to control buoyancy. They are divided into two subclasses: lobe-finned and ray-finned. Lobe-finned (also called fleshy-finned) fishes have muscular lobes supporting the pectoral and pelvic fins, and some kinds, including the late Devonian *Panderichthys* and *Eusthenopteron*, are believed to have used these to push their way through shallow waters. Ray-finned fishes, such as the Late Cretaceous *Hoplopteryx*, have fins stiffened by bony rays. An extinct class of fishes, known as the acanthodians or spiny sharks, lived during the Paleozoic era, and may possibly be related to the bony fishes. Their fins were protected by sharp spines. An example is the Middle Devonian *Cheiracanthus*.

DEVONIAN SPINY SHARK
(*Cheiracanthus sp.*); length: 12 in (30 cm)

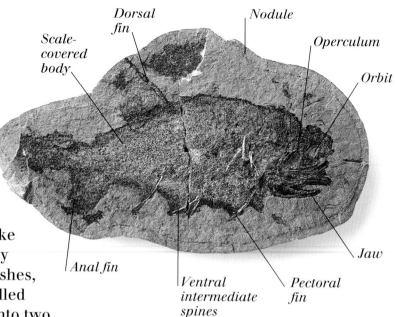

Dorsal fin

Nodule

Scale-covered body

Operculum

Orbit

Jaw

Anal fin

Ventral intermediate spines

Pectoral fin

EARLY EOCENE STINGRAY
A cartilaginous fish (*Heliobatis radians*)
Length: 12 in (30 cm)

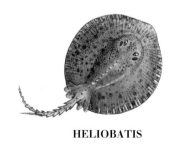

HELIOBATIS

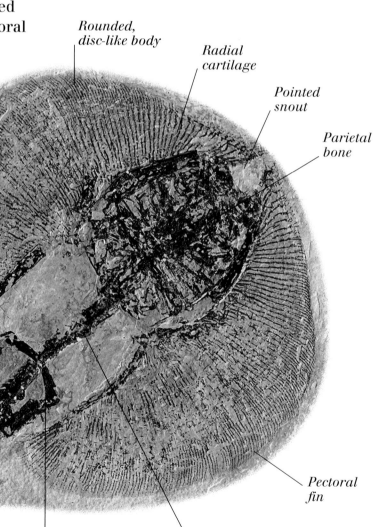

Rounded, disc-like body

Radial cartilage

Pointed snout

Parietal bone

Pelvic fin

Pelvic clasper

Pectoral fin

Tail spine

Tail vertebra

Pelvic girdle

Vertebra

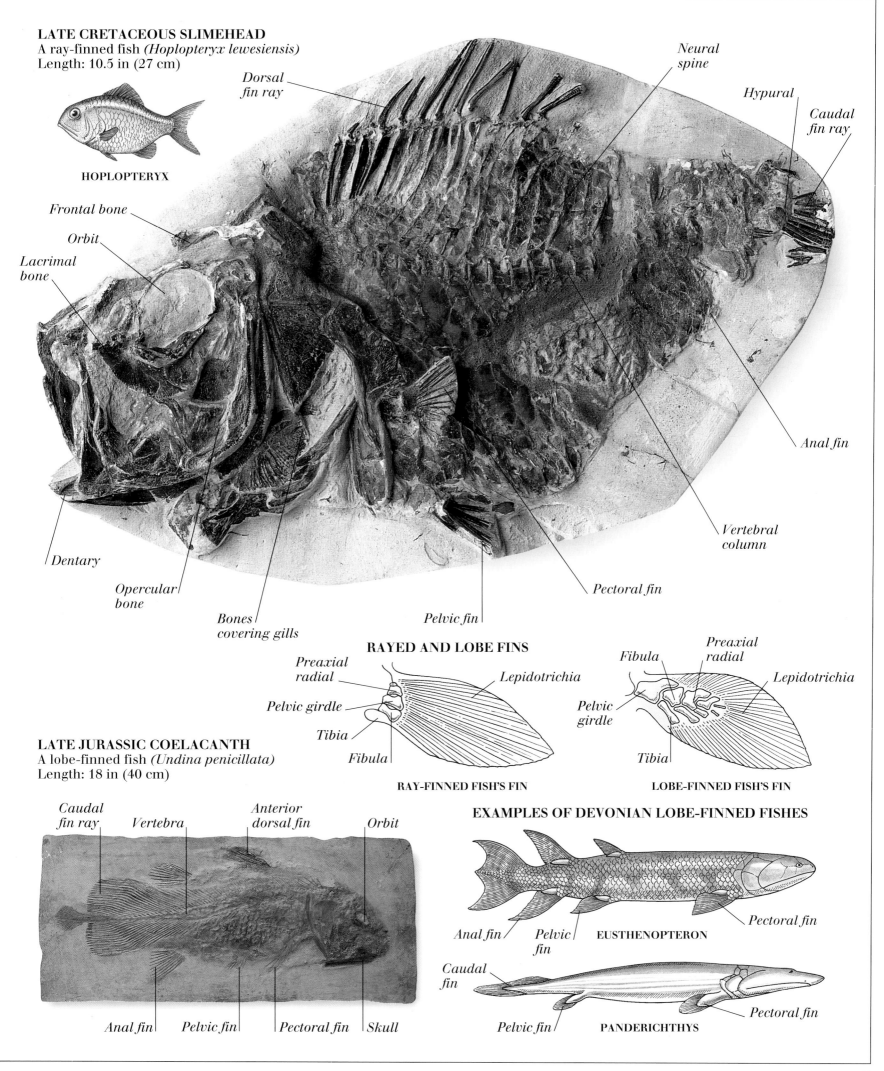

LATE CRETACEOUS SLIMEHEAD
A ray-finned fish *(Hoplopteryx lewesiensis)*
Length: 10.5 in (27 cm)

HOPLOPTERYX

Frontal bone

Orbit

Lacrimal bone

Dentary

Opercular bone

Bones covering gills

Dorsal fin ray

Neural spine

Hypural

Caudal fin ray

Anal fin

Vertebral column

Pectoral fin

Pelvic fin

RAYED AND LOBE FINS

Preaxial radial

Pelvic girdle

Tibia

Fibula

Lepidotrichia

RAY-FINNED FISH'S FIN

Fibula

Preaxial radial

Pelvic girdle

Tibia

Lepidotrichia

LOBE-FINNED FISH'S FIN

LATE JURASSIC COELACANTH
A lobe-finned fish *(Undina penicillata)*
Length: 18 in (40 cm)

Caudal fin ray

Vertebra

Anterior dorsal fin

Orbit

Anal fin

Pelvic fin

Pectoral fin

Skull

EXAMPLES OF DEVONIAN LOBE-FINNED FISHES

Anal fin

Pelvic fin

EUSTHENOPTERON

Pectoral fin

Caudal fin

Pelvic fin

PANDERICHTHYS

Pectoral fin

The rise of the amphibians

ABOUT 380 MILLION YEARS AGO in the Devonian period, lobe-finned fishes gave rise to vertebrates with limbs and digits, the first tetrapods. Their limbs evolved from fins, and the earliest tetrapods, such as *Acanthostega*, had legs that were adapted for paddling in shallow water. Others could perhaps have pulled themselves onto gently shelving shores. Like its lobe-finned ancestors, *Acanthostega* had a tail fin and internal gills, and could breathe air. The pattern of bones in its skull was similar to that of lobe-finned fishes. Early tetrapods had six or more digits on each hand or foot. By 330 million years ago, descendants of the early tetrapods had diversified into the amphibian and amniote lineages (see pp. 34–35) and also now-extinct forms that fall into neither of these categories. *Diplocaulus*, for example, was a bizarre early tetrapod that lived in rivers and lakes and was adapted for an aquatic life: the wide extensions on its skull are thought to have been used to direct its movement through the water. The large early amphibians (called temnospondyls) were sprawling and mostly aquatic animals, but the Early Permian *Eryops* is thought to have hunted its prey on land. The temnospondyls flourished from the Permian period (286–248 million years ago) to the middle of the Cretaceous (about 100 million years ago), when they became extinct. Their relatives, the lissamphibians—frogs, toads, newts, and others—are alive today.

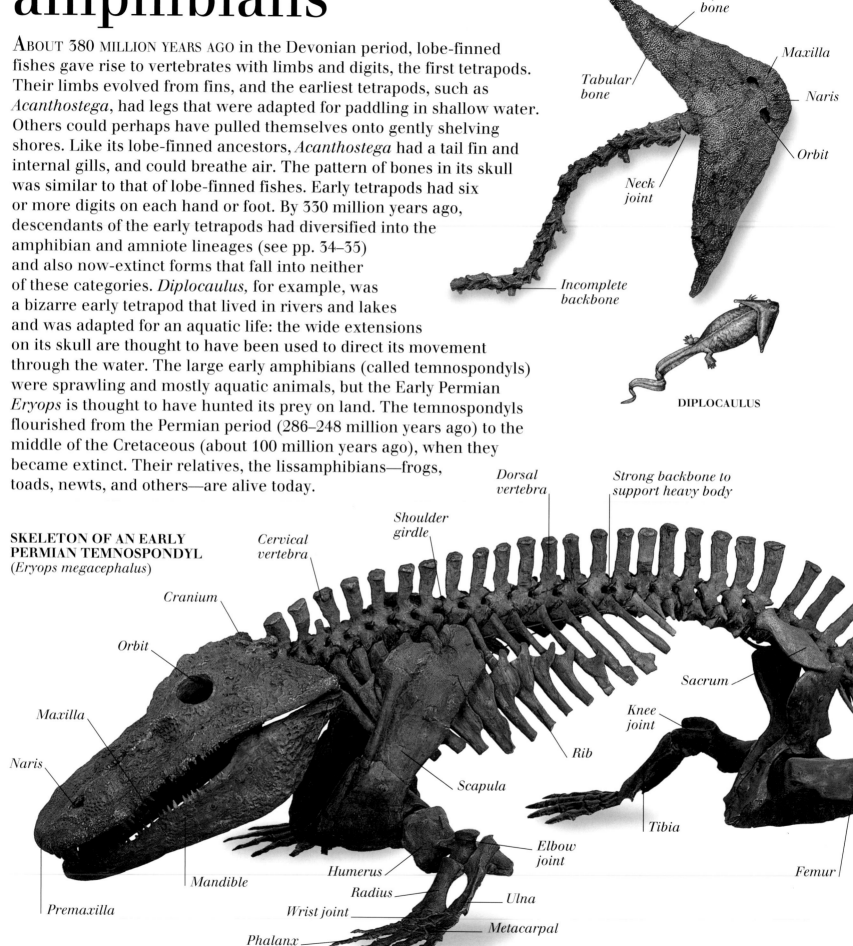

Squamosal bone

Maxilla

Tabular bone

Naris

Orbit

Neck joint

Incomplete backbone

DIPLOCAULUS

**SKELETON OF AN EARLY
PERMIAN TEMNOSPONDYL**
(*Eryops megacephalus*)

Dorsal vertebra

Strong backbone to support heavy body

Shoulder girdle

Cervical vertebra

Cranium

Orbit

Sacrum

Knee joint

Maxilla

Rib

Naris

Scapula

Tibia

Elbow joint

Humerus

Femur

Mandible

Radius

Ulna

Wrist joint

Metacarpal

Premaxilla

Phalanx

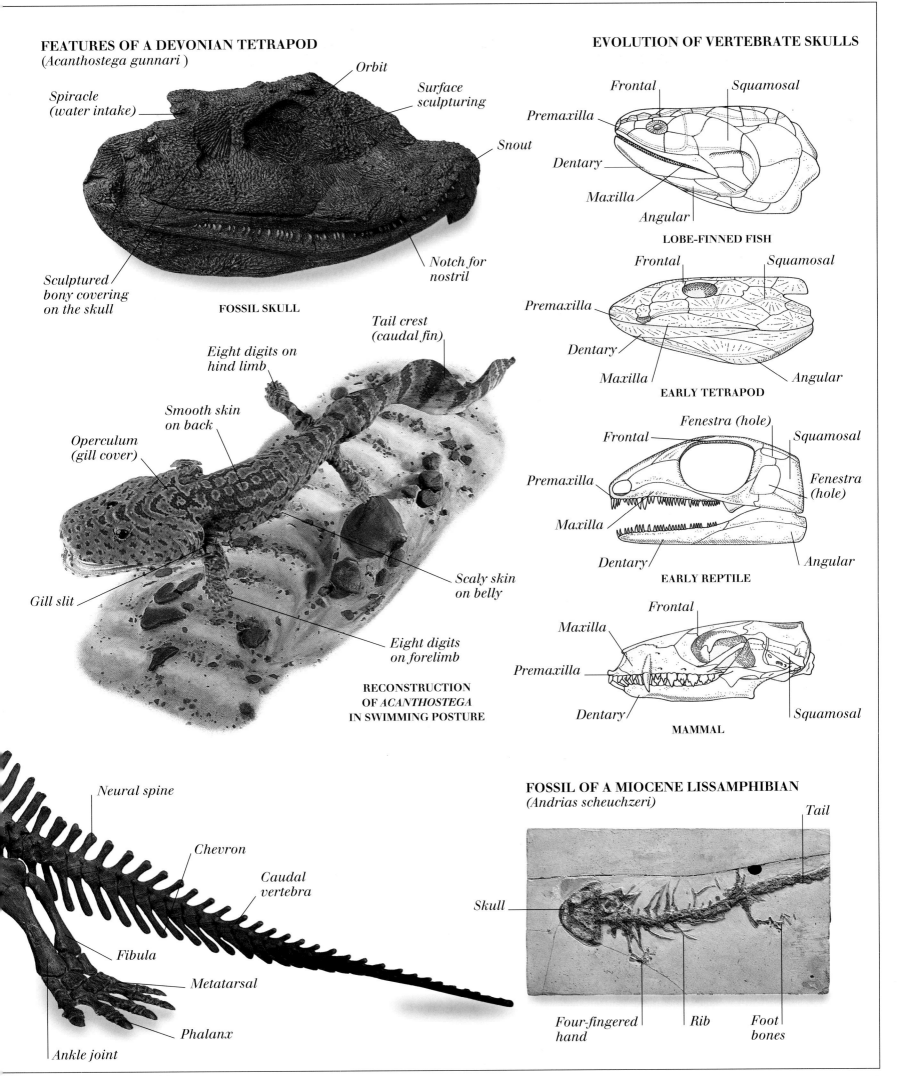

FEATURES OF A DEVONIAN TETRAPOD
(*Acanthostega gunnari*)

Spiracle
(water intake)

Orbit

Surface
sculpturing

Snout

Sculptured
bony covering
on the skull

Notch for
nostril

FOSSIL SKULL

Tail crest
(caudal fin)

Eight digits on
hind limb

Smooth skin
on back

Operculum
(gill cover)

Gill slit

Scaly skin
on belly

Eight digits
on forelimb

**RECONSTRUCTION
OF *ACANTHOSTEGA*
IN SWIMMING POSTURE**

EVOLUTION OF VERTEBRATE SKULLS

Frontal

Squamosal

Premaxilla

Dentary

Maxilla

Angular

LOBE-FINNED FISH

Frontal

Squamosal

Premaxilla

Dentary

Maxilla

Angular

EARLY TETRAPOD

Fenestra (hole)

Frontal

Squamosal

Premaxilla

Fenestra
(hole)

Maxilla

Dentary

Angular

EARLY REPTILE

Frontal

Maxilla

Premaxilla

Squamosal

Dentary

MAMMAL

Neural spine

Chevron

Caudal
vertebra

Fibula

Metatarsal

Phalanx

Ankle joint

FOSSIL OF A MIOCENE LISSAMPHIBIAN
(*Andrias scheuchzeri*)

Tail

Skull

Four-fingered
hand

Rib

Foot
bones

Primitive and synapsid reptiles

REPTILES WERE THE FIRST AMNIOTES. This group (reptiles, birds, and mammals) consists of the vertebrates that produce watertight eggs that hold the amniotic fluid which surrounds and protects the unborn young. Reptiles have been divided into three groupings according to the arrangement of openings on each side of their skulls behind the eyes. Primitive reptiles have no openings, synapsids have one, and diapsids (see pp. 36–37) have two. Primitive reptiles began as small, lizardlike insect-eaters. The Early Carboniferous animal *Westlothiana lizziae* may be the earliest known primitive reptile. Such primitive reptiles became extinct in the Late Triassic. The synapsids (also known as the mammal-like reptiles) lived from Late Carboniferous to Early Jurassic times. Early synapsids were cold-blooded creatures with a sprawling gait and posture, and included pelycosaurs. An example of these is *Edaphosaurus*, a 10-ft-long (3 m) herbivore with a skin sail on its back, held up by tall spines, which were upward projections from its backbone. Therapsids were an advanced group of synapsids. Herbivores included the 10-ft-long (3 m) *Sinokannemeyeria*, while carnivores included *Cynognathus*, which was 6 ft 6 in (2 m) long .

**SKELETON OF AN EARLY
TRIASSIC SYNAPSID REPTILE**
(*Sinokannemeyeria yinchiaoensis*)
Length: 10 ft (3 m)

Scapula

*Cervical
vertebra*

*Infratemporal
fenestra*

Cranium

Orbit

Naris

Maxilla

*Dentary
bone*

Mandible

*Elbow
joint*

Ulna

Wrist joint

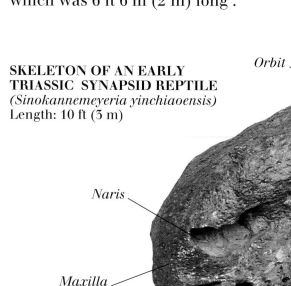

Metacarpal

Phalanx

SINOKANNEMEYERIA

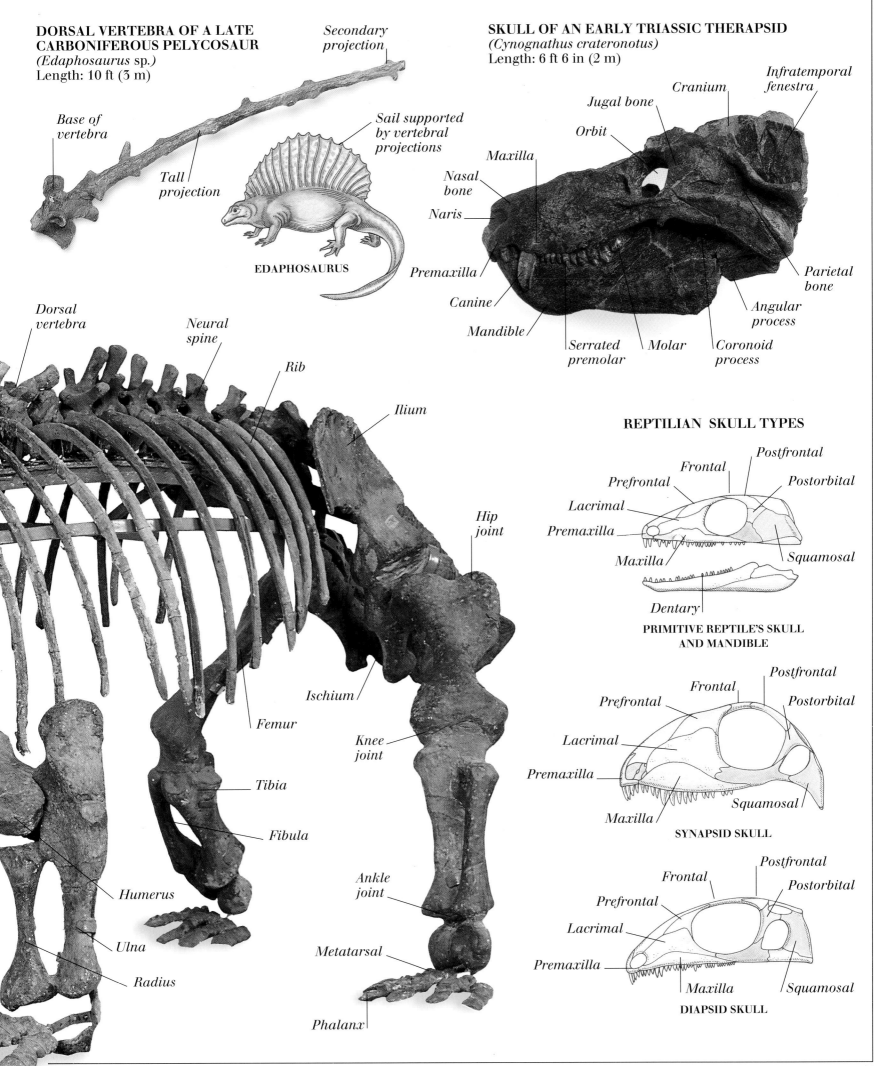

DORSAL VERTEBRA OF A LATE CARBONIFEROUS PELYCOSAUR
(*Edaphosaurus* sp.)
Length: 10 ft (3 m)

Secondary projection

Base of vertebra

Tall projection

Sail supported by vertebral projections

EDAPHOSAURUS

SKULL OF AN EARLY TRIASSIC THERAPSID
(*Cynognathus crateronotus*)
Length: 6 ft 6 in (2 m)

Cranium

Jugal bone

Orbit

Infratemporal fenestra

Maxilla

Nasal bone

Naris

Premaxilla

Canine

Mandible

Serrated premolar

Molar

Coronoid process

Angular process

Parietal bone

Dorsal vertebra

Neural spine

Rib

Ilium

Hip joint

Ischium

Femur

Knee joint

Tibia

Fibula

Humerus

Ulna

Radius

Ankle joint

Metatarsal

Phalanx

REPTILIAN SKULL TYPES

Frontal

Postfrontal

Prefrontal

Postorbital

Lacrimal

Premaxilla

Maxilla

Squamosal

Dentary

PRIMITIVE REPTILE'S SKULL AND MANDIBLE

Postfrontal

Frontal

Prefrontal

Postorbital

Lacrimal

Premaxilla

Maxilla

Squamosal

SYNAPSID SKULL

Postfrontal

Frontal

Postorbital

Prefrontal

Lacrimal

Premaxilla

Maxilla

Squamosal

DIAPSID SKULL

Marine reptiles

THE FIRST DIAPSID REPTILES evolved some 300 million years ago in the Late Carboniferous. All modern reptiles except turtles, and many extinct groups as well, evolved from these animals. Among their extinct descendants were various swimming reptiles of the Mesozoic era (248–65 million years ago). In the Triassic period (248–208 million years ago) there were two major types of sea reptiles. The slender nothosaurs swam by thrusting water backward with their tails, and fed by spearing fish with sharp, interlocking teeth. The sturdy placodonts fed on shellfish, harvesting them with shovel-like front teeth and crushing them against specialized back teeth. By the Jurassic period (208–144 million years ago), these groups had died out, to be replaced by plesiosaurs and ichthyosaurs, whose limbs had evolved into flippers. Short-necked plesiosaurs were known as pliosaurs. The larger pliosaurs hunted ichthyosaurs—streamlined, dolphinlike reptiles, with fins, flippers, and long, narrow jaws. By the close of the Mesozoic era, the ichthyosaurs had been replaced by mosasaurs—sea lizards with paddle-shaped limbs and sharp-toothed jaws.

NINETEENTH-CENTURY RECONSTRUCTION OF A MESOZOIC SEASCAPE

Fishlike tail

Streamlined body

Finlike flipper

TYLOSAURUS
A Late Cretaceous mosasaur
Length: 19 ft 6 in (6 m)

Rib

Dorsal vertebra

Sacral vertebra

Sacrum

SKELETON OF A LATE JURASSIC PLESIOSAUR
(Cryptoclidus eurymerus)
Length: 13 ft (4 m)

Neural spine

Ilium

Ischium

Chevron

Caudal vertebra

Phalanx

Tarsal

Femur

Pelvic girdle

Belly rib

Sternum

Humerus

Carpal

Phalanx

CRYPTOCLIDUS

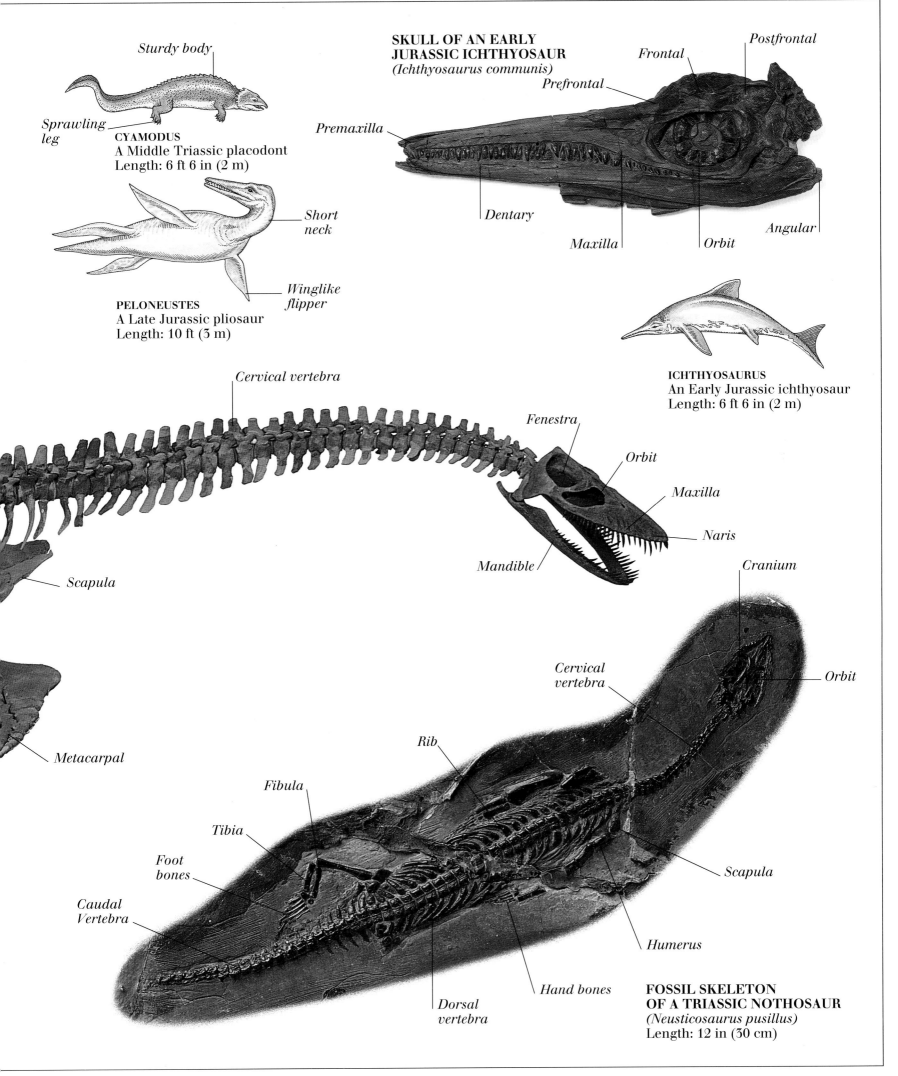

Sturdy body

Sprawling
leg

CYAMODUS
A Middle Triassic placodont
Length: 6 ft 6 in (2 m)

Short
neck

Winglike
flipper

PELONEUSTES
A Late Jurassic pliosaur
Length: 10 ft (3 m)

**SKULL OF AN EARLY
JURASSIC ICHTHYOSAUR**
(Ichthyosaurus communis)

Frontal

Postfrontal

Prefrontal

Premaxilla

Dentary

Maxilla

Orbit

Angular

ICHTHYOSAURUS
An Early Jurassic ichthyosaur
Length: 6 ft 6 in (2 m)

Cervical vertebra

Fenestra

Orbit

Maxilla

Naris

Mandible

Scapula

Metacarpal

Cranium

Cervical
vertebra

Orbit

Rib

Fibula

Tibia

Foot
bones

Caudal
Vertebra

Scapula

Humerus

Hand bones

**FOSSIL SKELETON
OF A TRIASSIC NOTHOSAUR**
(Neusticosaurus pusillus)
Length: 12 in (30 cm)

Dorsal
vertebra

Relatives of the dinosaurs

THE ARCHOSAUROMORPHS were a diapsid (see p. 34) reptile group that included rhynchosaurs and archosaurs—diapsids with an extra opening in the skull ahead of each eye. Archosaurs dominated life on land throughout much of the Mesozoic era (248–65 million years ago). In the Triassic period (248–208 million years ago), archosaurs diversified into four sub-groups: "thecodonts," dinosaurs, pterosaurs, and crocodilians. "Thecodonts," the first to evolve, are given in quotation marks because there is some doubt that they formed a closely related group. The Early Triassic thecodont *Euparkeria* was partially bipedal; it could tuck in its knees and rear up on its hind legs to run. In the Late Triassic, thecodonts gave rise to dinosaurs and pterosaurs. Pterosaurs were flying reptiles with skin-covered wings. Crocodilians included *Deinosuchus*, possibly the largest-ever crocodile, living in the Late Cretaceous (97.5–65 million years ago). All thecodonts died out by the end of the Triassic; the dinosaurs and pterosaurs lived until the end of the Cretaceous.

FOSSIL OF A LATE JURASSIC PTEROSAUR
(Pterodactylus kochi)

PTERODACTYLUS

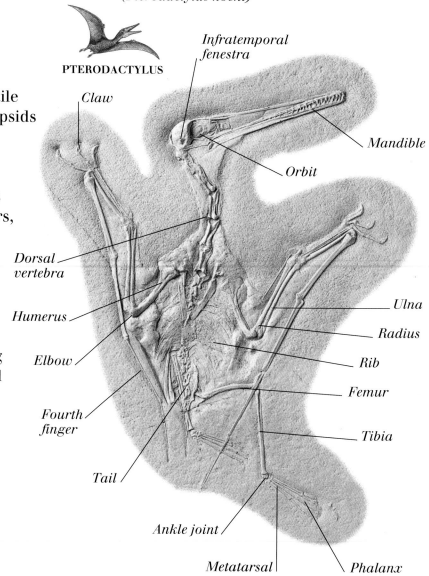

- Infratemporal fenestra
- Claw
- Mandible
- Orbit
- Dorsal vertebra
- Humerus
- Ulna
- Radius
- Elbow
- Rib
- Femur
- Fourth finger
- Tibia
- Tail
- Ankle joint
- Metatarsal
- Phalanx

FEATURES OF AN EARLY TRIASSIC THECODONT
(Euparkeria capensis)
Length: 20 in (50 cm)

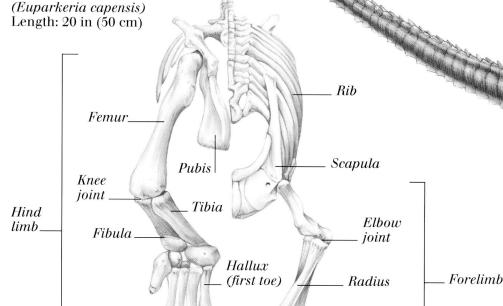

- Femur
- Rib
- Pubis
- Scapula
- Knee joint
- Tibia
- Hind limb
- Elbow joint
- Fibula
- Hallux (first toe)
- Radius
- Forelimb
- Metatarsal
- Ulna
- Phalanx

HIND LIMB AND FORELIMB OF *EUPARKERIA*

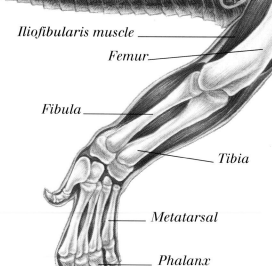

- Caudal vertebra
- Iliofibularis muscle
- Femur
- Fibula
- Tibia
- Metatarsal
- Phalanx

EXAMPLES OF ARCHOSAUROMORPHS

ERYTHROSUCHUS
A thecodont
Length: 14 ft 9 in (4.5 m)

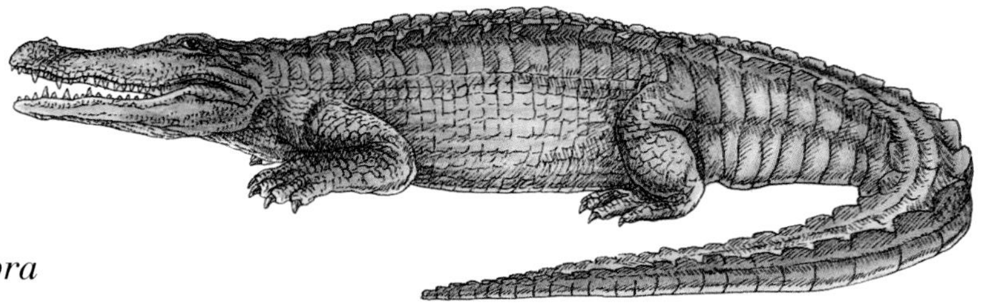

DEINOSUCHUS a crocodilian
Length: 52 ft 6 in (16 m)

SKELETON OF SCAPHONYX

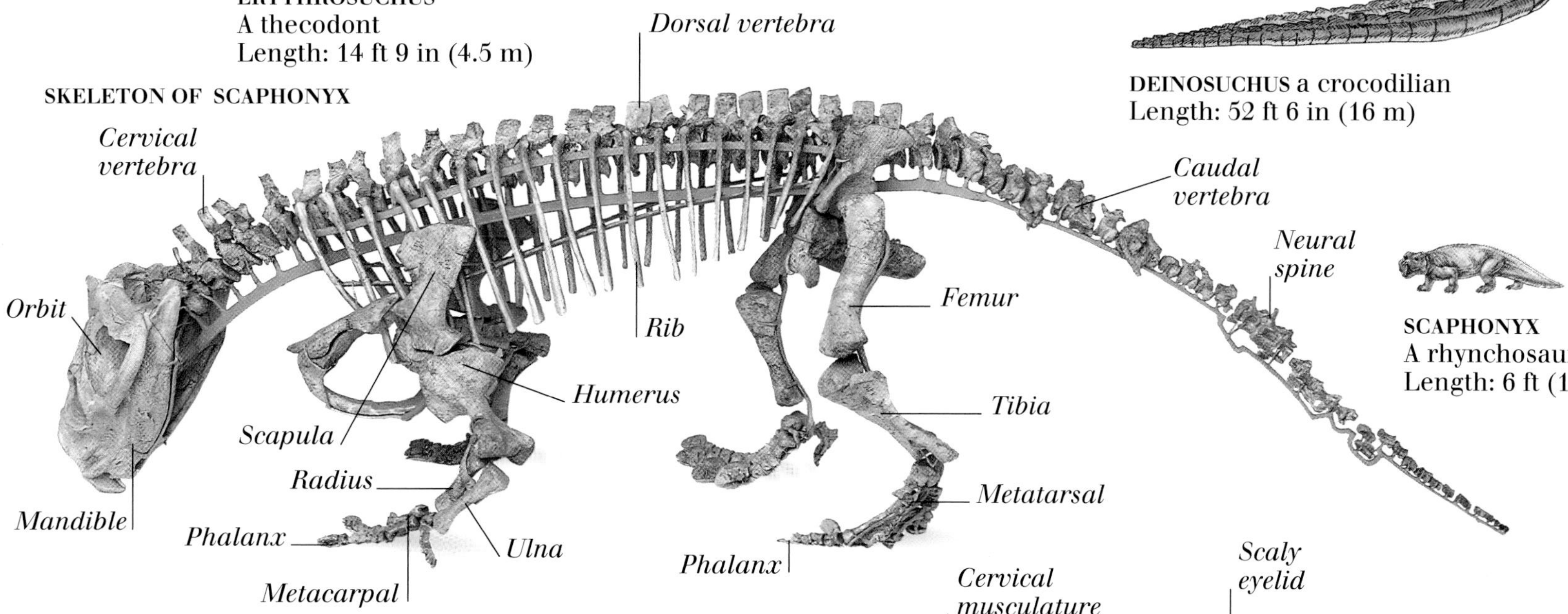

Cervical vertebra

Dorsal vertebra

Caudal vertebra

Neural spine

SCAPHONYX
A rhynchosaur
Length: 6 ft (1.8 m)

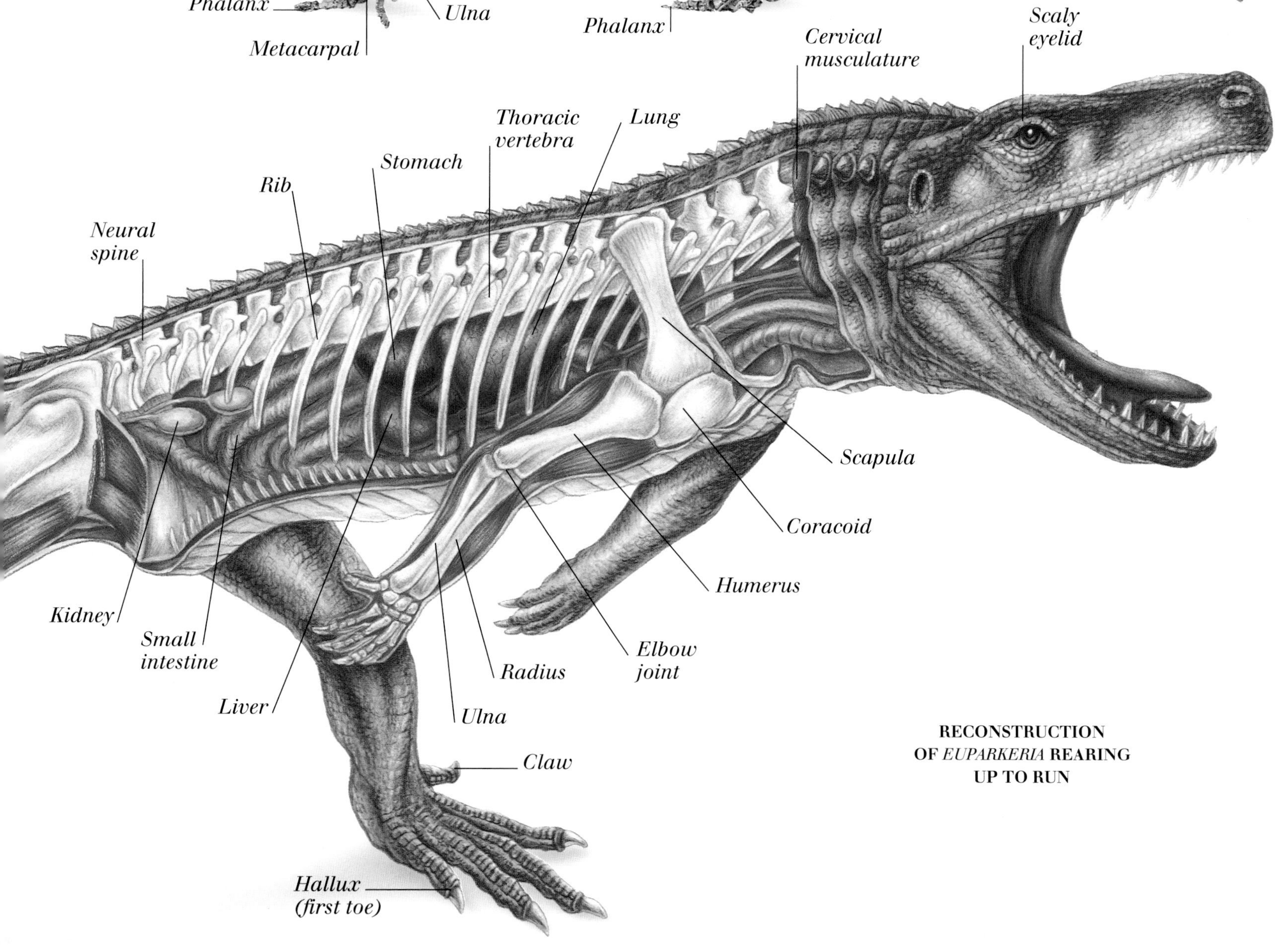

Orbit

Femur

Rib

Humerus

Tibia

Scapula

Radius

Metatarsal

Mandible

Phalanx

Ulna

Phalanx

Metacarpal

Scaly eyelid

Cervical musculature

Thoracic vertebra

Lung

Stomach

Rib

Neural spine

Scapula

Coracoid

Humerus

Kidney

Small intestine

Radius

Elbow joint

Liver

Ulna

RECONSTRUCTION OF *EUPARKERIA* REARING UP TO RUN

Claw

Hallux (first toe)

39

Saurischian dinosaurs

DINOSAURS WERE THE DOMINANT LAND ANIMALS from Late Triassic to Late Cretaceous times (about 225–65 million years ago). They are classified as a subdivision of the archosaurs (see pages 38–39), distinguished by their upright stance (unlike that of most archosaurs) and various details of skull and limb bones. Dinosaurs are divided into saurischians, in which the pubes (a pair of bones in the hip girdle) typically slanted forward, and ornithischians, in which the same bones slanted back. Saurischians in turn are divided into theropods and sauropodomorphs. Theropods, which included all predatory dinosaurs, ranged in size from the chicken-sized *Compsognathus* to the 49-ft-long (15 m), sail-backed *Spinosaurus*. Other examples are *Tyrannosaurus rex* and the birdlike *Avimimus*. Sauropodomorphs include the largest land animals ever to have lived, and fall into two groups: the prosauropods and their immense successors, the sauropods, such as the 69-ft-long (21 m) *Apatosaurus*.

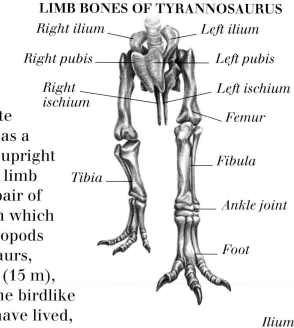

FRONT VIEW OF HIP GIRDLE AND LIMB BONES OF TYRANNOSAURUS

Right ilium
Left ilium
Right pubis
Left pubis
Right ischium
Left ischium
Femur
Tibia
Fibula
Ankle joint
Foot

EXAMPLES OF SAURISCHIAN DINOSAURS

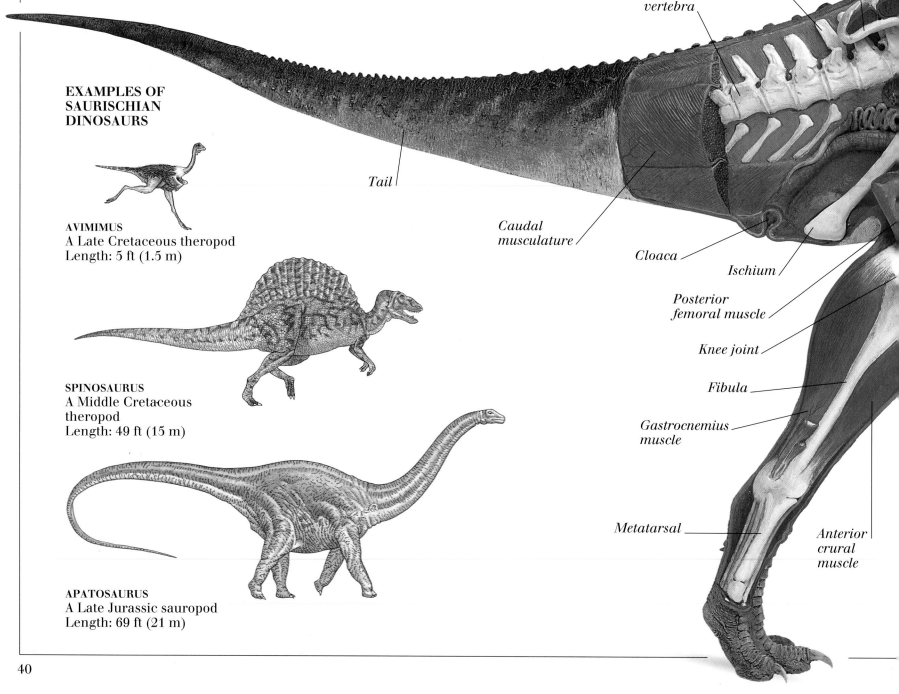

AVIMIMUS
A Late Cretaceous theropod
Length: 5 ft (1.5 m)

SPINOSAURUS
A Middle Cretaceous theropod
Length: 49 ft (15 m)

APATOSAURUS
A Late Jurassic sauropod
Length: 69 ft (21 m)

Ilium
Neural spine
Caudal vertebra
Caudal musculature
Tail
Cloaca
Ischium
Posterior femoral muscle
Knee joint
Fibula
Gastrocnemius muscle
Metatarsal
Anterior crural muscle

COMPARISON OF DINOSAUR HIP BONES

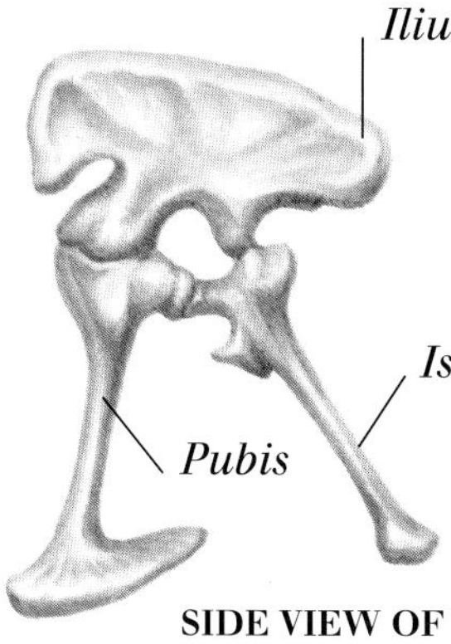

Ilium

Prepubis

Ilium

Ischium

Ischium

Pubis

Pubis

**SIDE VIEW OF
SAURISCHIAN HIP
GIRDLE**

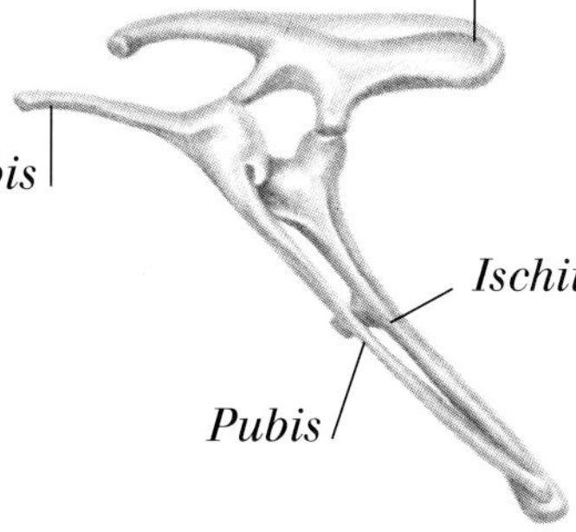

**SIDE VIEW OF
ORNITHISCHIAN HIP
GIRDLE**

**ANATOMY OF A
MIDDLE CRETACEOUS THEROPOD**
(Carnotaurus sastrei)
Length: 25 ft (7.6 m)

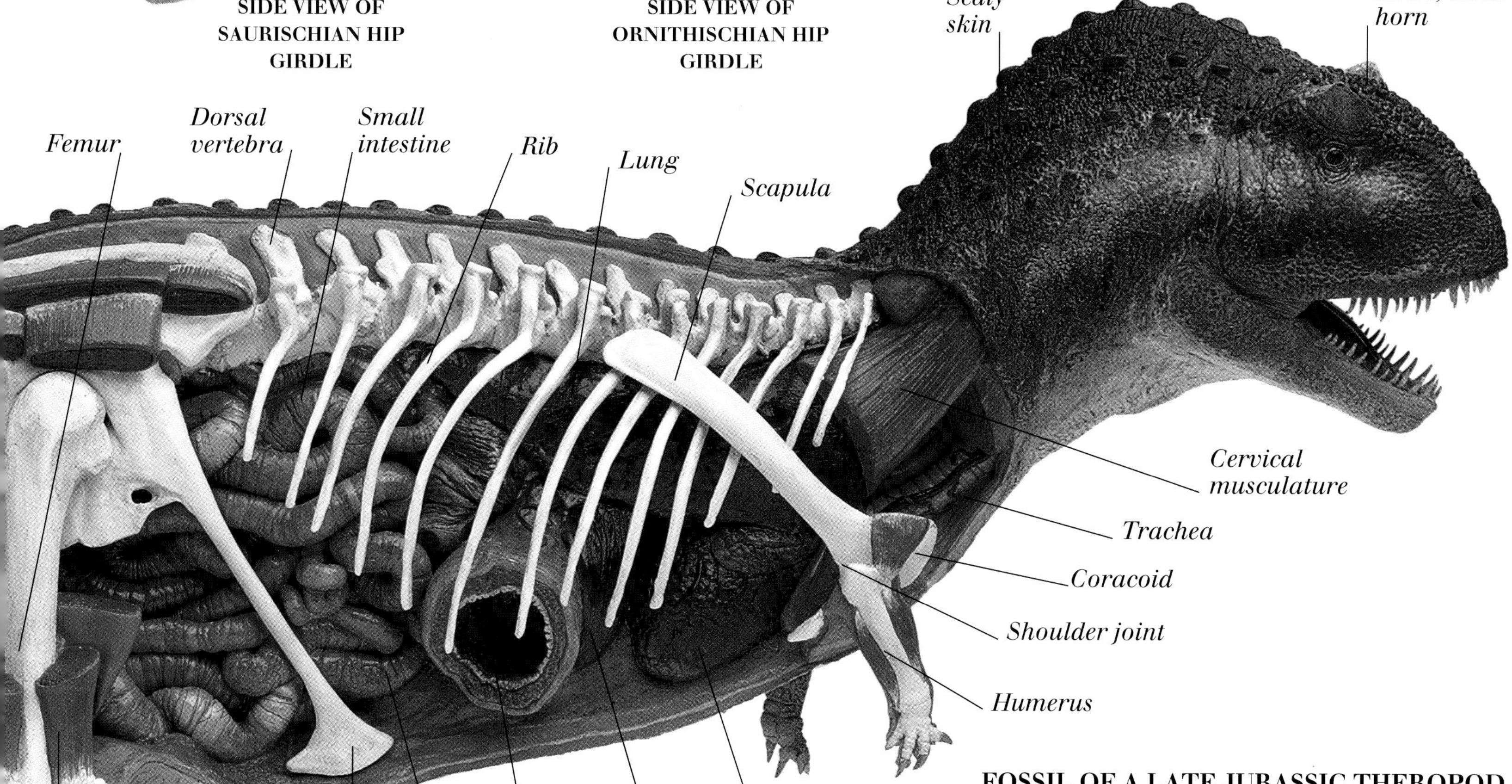

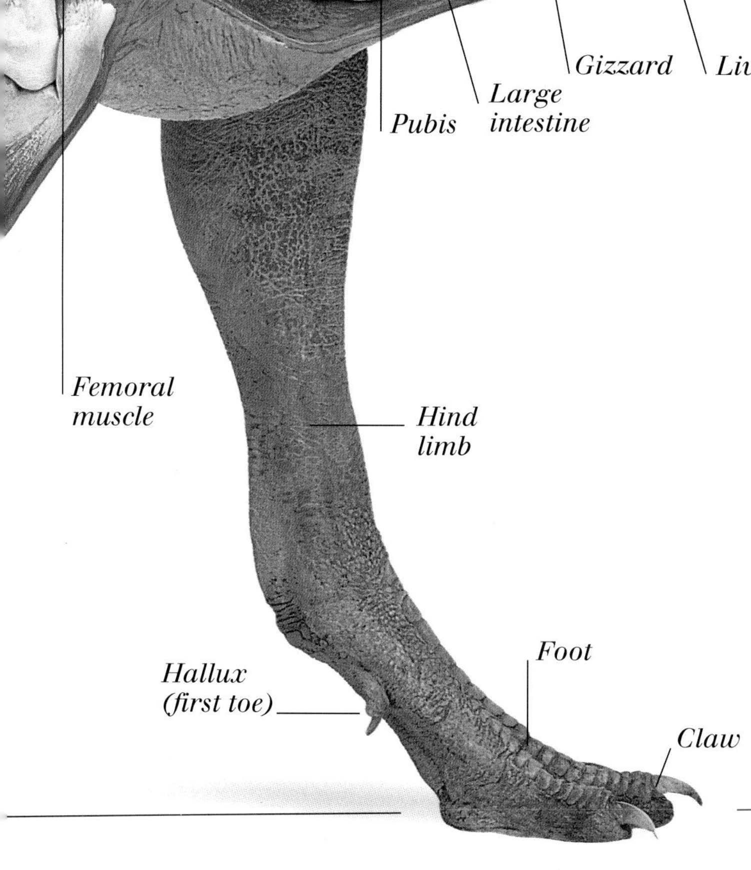

*Prominent
armored scale*

*Scaly
skin*

*Short, stout
horn*

Femur

*Dorsal
vertebra*

*Small
intestine*

Rib

Lung

Scapula

*Cervical
musculature*

Trachea

Coracoid

Shoulder joint

Humerus

Gizzard

Liver

Heart

Pubis

*Large
intestine*

FOSSIL OF A LATE JURASSIC THEROPOD
(Compsognathus longipes)
Length: 24 in (60 cm)

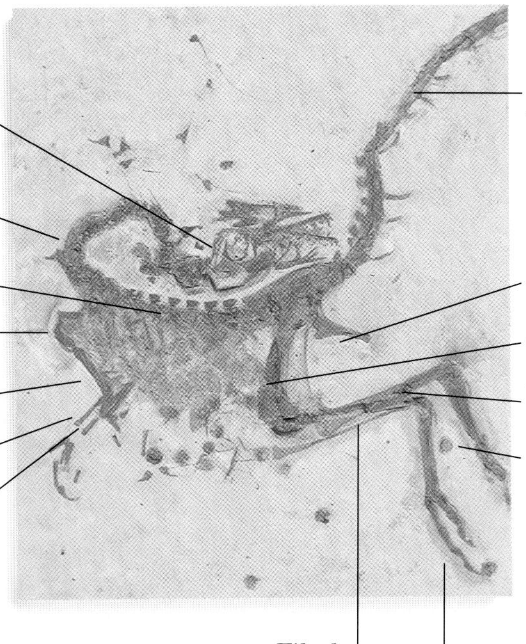

Orbit

*Caudal
vertebra*

Cervical vertebra

Dorsal vertebra

Ischium

Scapula

Femur

Humerus

Tibia

Radius

Metatarsal

Ulna

*Femoral
muscle*

*Hind
limb*

*Hallux
(first toe)*

Foot

Claw

Fibula

Phalanx

Ornithischian dinosaurs

TUOJIANGOSAURUS
A thyreophoran

THE ORNITHISCHIANS WERE HERBIVOROUS dinosaurs, with teeth and jaws adapted to their diet. Most had a toothless beak for cropping leaves, cheek pouches in which to store them, and cheek teeth for chewing them. There are three ornithischian suborders: ornithopods, thyreophorans, and marginocephalians. Ornithopods included some species that ran on their hind legs, at least for some of the time. Among these was the hadrosaur *Parasaurolophus*, which had a backswept bony head crest containing a trombonelike airway that allowed the 33-ft-long (10 m) herbivore to emit loud calls. Thyreophorans comprised the stegosaurs and ankylosaurs. Stegosaurs, such as the 23-ft-long (7 m) *Tuojiangosaurus,* bore two rows of spikes or plates jutting up from the neck, back, and tail. Ankylosaurs ranged in size from the 10-ft-long (3 m) *Minmi* to the heavily armored, 23-ft-long (7 m) *Euoplocephalus*, which possessed a bony tail club. Marginocephalians had a narrow shelf or deep bony frill at the back of the skull, and comprised two groups: pachycephalosaurs, such as *Stegoceras*, and ceratopsians, such as *Psittacosaurus* and *Protoceratops*, 6 ft (1.8 m) long. The largest ceratopsian was *Triceratops*, a three-horned, rhinoceros-like dinosaur measuring 29 ft 6 in (9 m) in length.

SKULLS OF MARGINOCEPHALIANS

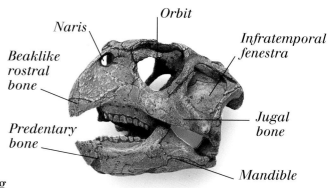

Naris
Orbit
Beaklike rostral bone
Infratemporal fenestra
Predentary bone
Jugal bone
Mandible

PSITTACOSAURUS SKULL

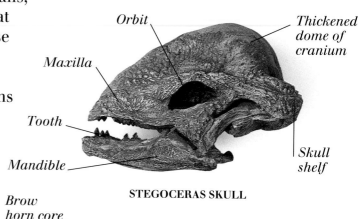

Orbit
Thickened dome of cranium
Maxilla
Tooth
Mandible
Skull shelf

STEGOCERAS SKULL

Brow horn core
Parietosquamosal frill
Nose horn core
Orbit
Naris
Rostral bone
Infratemporal fenestra
Mandible

TRICERATOPS SKULL

SKELETON OF A LATE CRETACEOUS MARGINOCEPHALIAN
(Protoceratops andrewsi)
Length: 6 ft (1.8 m)

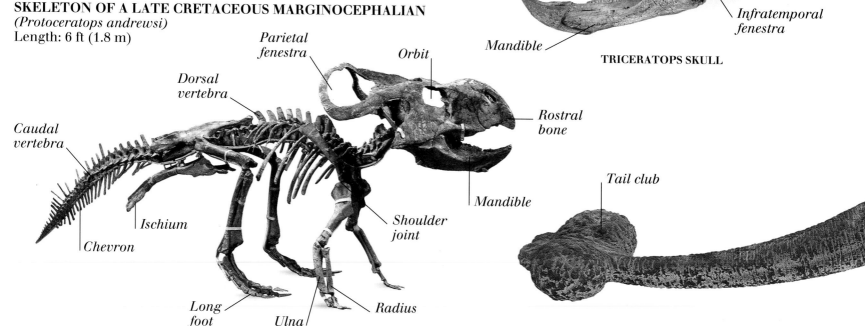

Parietal fenestra
Orbit
Dorsal vertebra
Rostral bone
Caudal vertebra
Mandible
Ischium
Shoulder joint
Chevron
Tail club
Long foot
Ulna
Radius

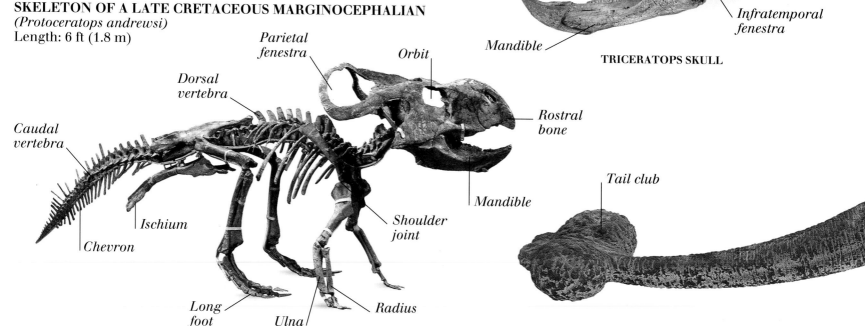

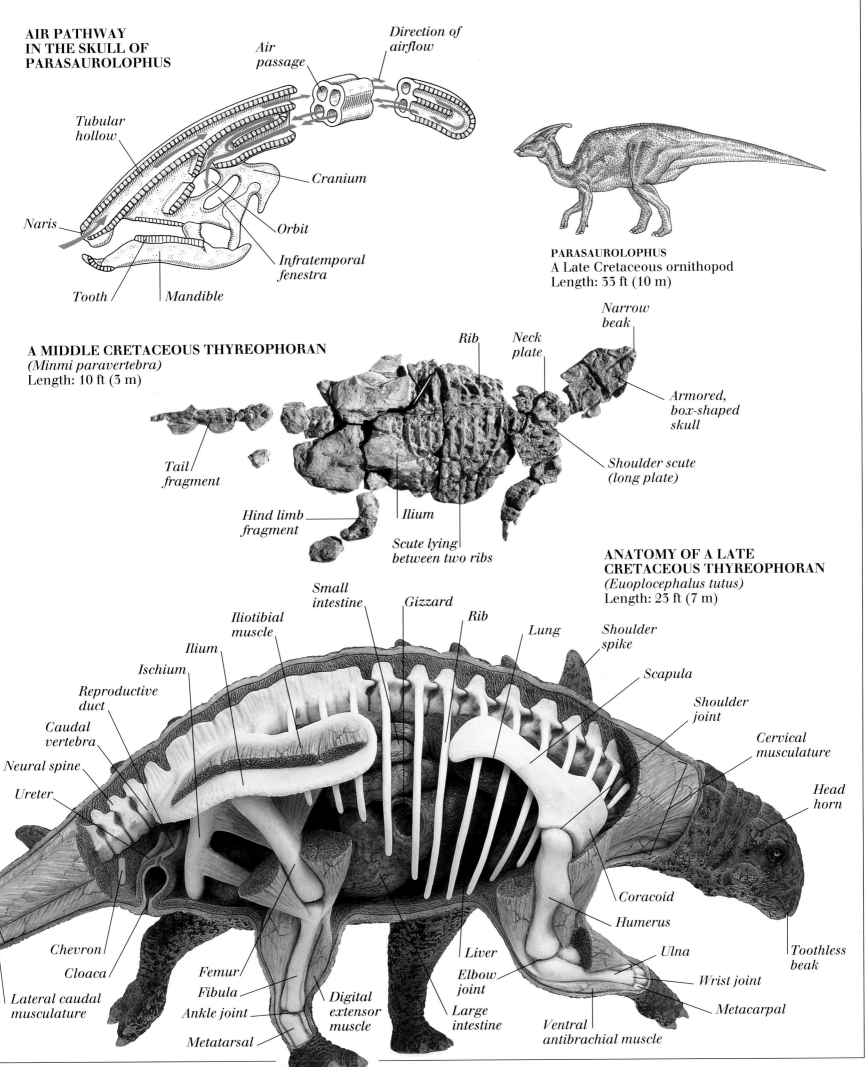

AIR PATHWAY IN THE SKULL OF PARASAUROLOPHUS

Air passage

Direction of airflow

Tubular hollow

Cranium

Naris

Orbit

Infratemporal fenestra

Tooth

Mandible

PARASAUROLOPHUS
A Late Cretaceous ornithopod
Length: 33 ft (10 m)

A MIDDLE CRETACEOUS THYREOPHORAN
(Minmi paravertebra)
Length: 10 ft (3 m)

Rib

Neck plate

Narrow beak

Armored, box-shaped skull

Tail fragment

Shoulder scute (long plate)

Hind limb fragment

Ilium

Scute lying between two ribs

ANATOMY OF A LATE CRETACEOUS THYREOPHORAN
(Euoplocephalus tutus)
Length: 23 ft (7 m)

Small intestine

Gizzard

Rib

Lung

Shoulder spike

Iliotibial muscle

Scapula

Ilium

Shoulder joint

Ischium

Cervical musculature

Reproductive duct

Caudal vertebra

Neural spine

Ureter

Head horn

Chevron

Coracoid

Cloaca

Humerus

Lateral caudal musculature

Femur

Liver

Ulna

Toothless beak

Fibula

Elbow joint

Wrist joint

Ankle joint

Digital extensor muscle

Large intestine

Metacarpal

Metatarsal

Ventral antibrachial muscle

The earliest birds

THE EARLIEST KNOWN BIRD was *Archaeopteryx*, which was the size of a modern crow and lived in the Late Jurassic, 150 million years ago. It is believed to be descended from the maniraptorans, a group of small theropod dinosaurs with particularly lightweight, agile bodies. The main apparent difference was that *Archaeopteryx* was covered in feathers. So close is the similarity in other respects that it is claimed that birds are living, flying dinosaurs. *Archaeopteryx* had the small, sharp teeth, the clawed fingers, and the long, bony tail core of a maniraptoran. Teeth persisted in some birds of the Cretaceous period (144–65 million years ago): *Ichthyornis*, a bird resembling a modern tern, and *Hesperornis*, a large diving bird. No toothed bird has existed since the Cretaceous, the nearest equivalent being the "bony-toothed" birds of the Tertiary period (65–2 million years ago) such as *Osteodontornis*. In place of true teeth, these birds had sharp projections of the bone in each mandible. Some birds of the Late Cretaceous, such as *Patagopteryx*, lost the power of flight. In some parts of the world during the Tertiary, flightless land birds rivaled carnivorous mammals as the leading predators. *Phorusrhacus*, an example from 20 million years ago in the Early Miocene, was a powerful hunter on the plains of southern South America.

ICHTHYORNIS

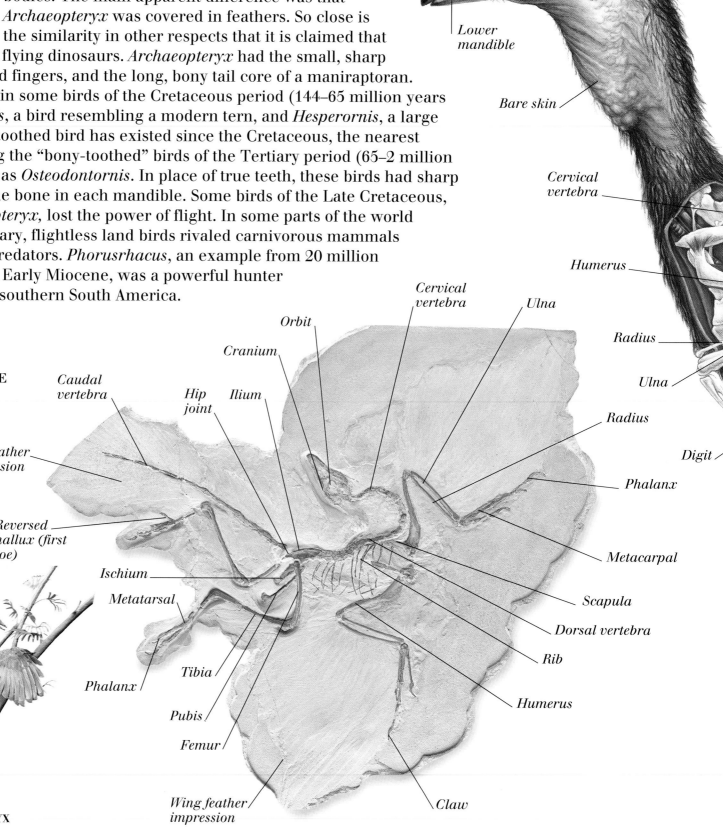

Scaly eye ring

Upper mandible

Ear

Lower mandible

Bare skin

Cervical vertebra

Humerus

Radius

Ulna

FOSSIL OF A LATE JURASSIC BIRD
(Archaeopteryx lithographica)

Caudal vertebra

Cranium

Orbit

Cervical vertebra

Ulna

Hip joint

Ilium

Tail feather impression

Radius

Digit

Reversed hallux (first toe)

Phalanx

Ischium

Metacarpal

Metatarsal

Scapula

Dorsal vertebra

Rib

Phalanx

Tibia

Humerus

Pubis

Femur

Wing feather impression

Claw

ARCHAEOPTERYX

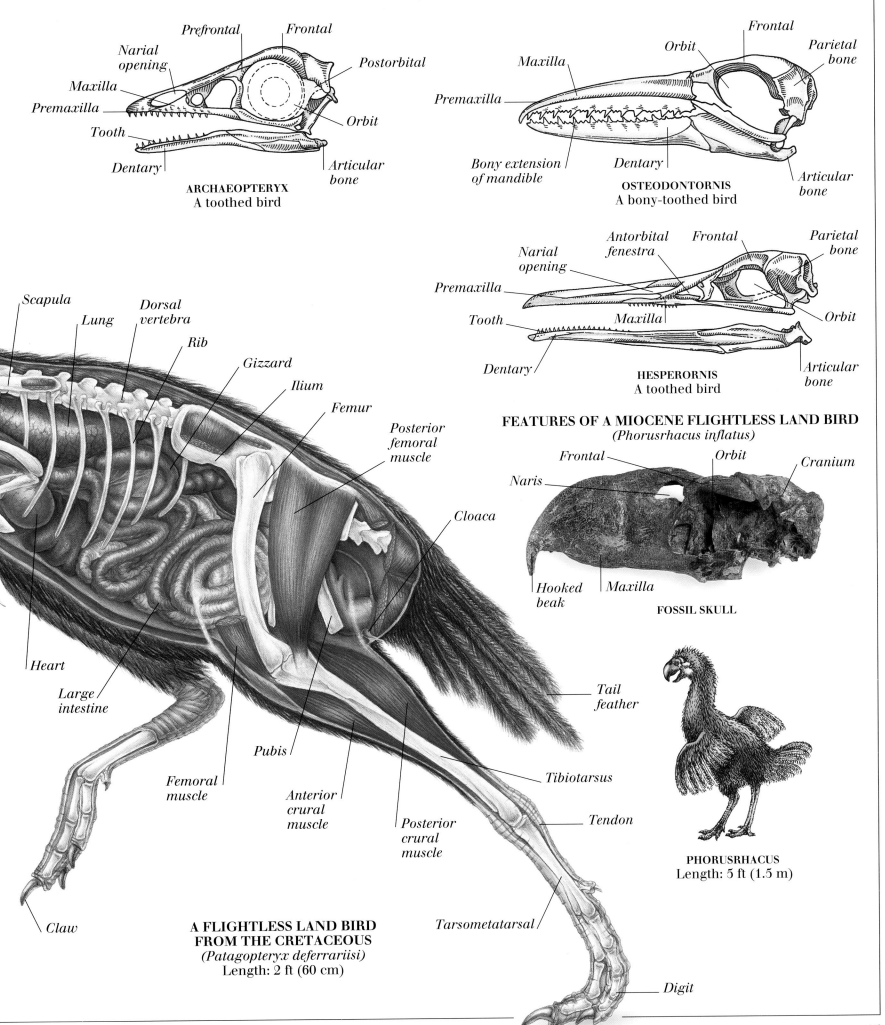

SKULLS OF TOOTHED AND BONY-TOOTHED BIRDS

Prefrontal

Frontal

Narial
opening

Maxilla

Premaxilla

Tooth

Dentary

Postorbital

Orbit

Articular
bone

ARCHAEOPTERYX
A toothed bird

Frontal

Orbit

Parietal
bone

Maxilla

Premaxilla

Bony extension
of mandible

Dentary

Articular
bone

OSTEODONTORNIS
A bony-toothed bird

Antorbital
fenestra

Frontal

Parietal
bone

Narial
opening

Premaxilla

Tooth

Maxilla

Dentary

Orbit

Articular
bone

HESPERORNIS
A toothed bird

FEATURES OF A MIOCENE FLIGHTLESS LAND BIRD
(Phorusrhacus inflatus)

Frontal

Naris

Orbit

Cranium

Hooked
beak

Maxilla

FOSSIL SKULL

Scapula

Lung

Dorsal
vertebra

Rib

Gizzard

Ilium

Femur

Posterior
femoral
muscle

Cloaca

Heart

Large
intestine

Pubis

Femoral
muscle

Anterior
crural
muscle

Posterior
crural
muscle

Tail
feather

Tibiotarsus

Tendon

Claw

**A FLIGHTLESS LAND BIRD
FROM THE CRETACEOUS**
(Patagopteryx deferrariisi)
Length: 2 ft (60 cm)

Tarsometatarsal

PHORUSRHACUS
Length: 5 ft (1.5 m)

Digit

Primitive mammals

DIPROTODON

Mammals are warm-blooded, often hairy vertebrates whose females produce milk for their young. They appeared about 220 million years ago, in the Late Triassic, soon after the first dinosaurs. Fossils of early mammals can be distinguished from those of therapsid reptiles (see pp. 34–35) by distinctive bones of the jaw and middle ear. The earliest mammals resembled shrews and developed multicusped teeth (with more than one cusp or point), which sheared through food when they chewed. One group of primitive mammals, the monotremes, laid eggs and are represented today by the platypus and the spiny anteaters. Most fossil and living mammals belong to the subclass Theria, which give birth to live young. Before the death of the dinosaurs (65 million years ago), two groups of Theria appeared, the marsupials (pouched mammals) which produce tiny, underdeveloped young, and the placentals which give birth to well-developed babies, nourished in their mother's womb by a placenta. Pleistocene marsupials included the hippopotamus-sized *Diprotodon* from Australia, and the still-living opossums (family Didelphidae) from the Americas. Extinct Pleistocene placentals included the ground sloth *Megatherium*, and the giant armadillo *Glyptodon*, both from South America. Both are edentates, a primitive group that includes modern armadillos, anteaters, and sloths.

PLEISTOCENE PLACENTAL
(Megatherium americanum)
Length: 19 ft 6 in (6 m)

FEATURES OF A PLEISTOCENE EDENTATE
(Glyptodon reticulatus)
Length: 6 ft 6 in (2 m)

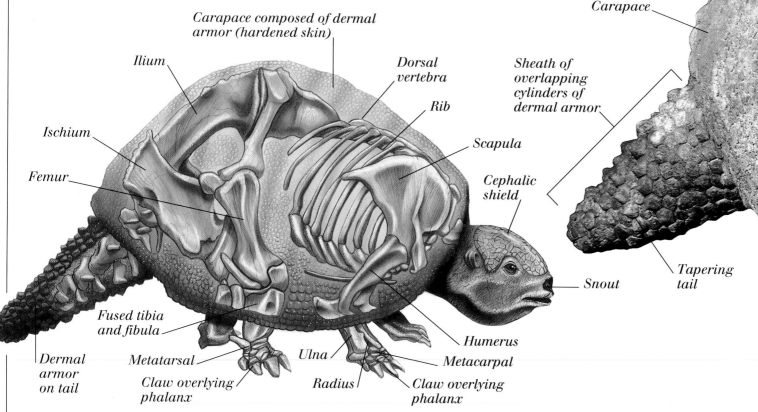

Carapace composed of dermal armor (hardened skin)

Ilium

Dorsal vertebra

Rib

Ischium

Scapula

Femur

Cephalic shield

Carapace

Sheath of overlapping cylinders of dermal armor

Fused tibia and fibula

Snout

Tapering tail

Dermal armor on tail

Metatarsal

Ulna

Humerus

Metacarpal

Claw overlying phalanx

Radius

Claw overlying phalanx

INTERNAL VIEW SHOWING SKELETON

EXAMPLES OF PRIMITIVE MAMMALS

PLEISTOCENE MARSUPIAL
(Didelphis albiventris)
Length: 12 in (30 cm)

JURASSIC EUPANTOTHERE
(Amblotherium pusillum)
Length: 10 in (25 cm)

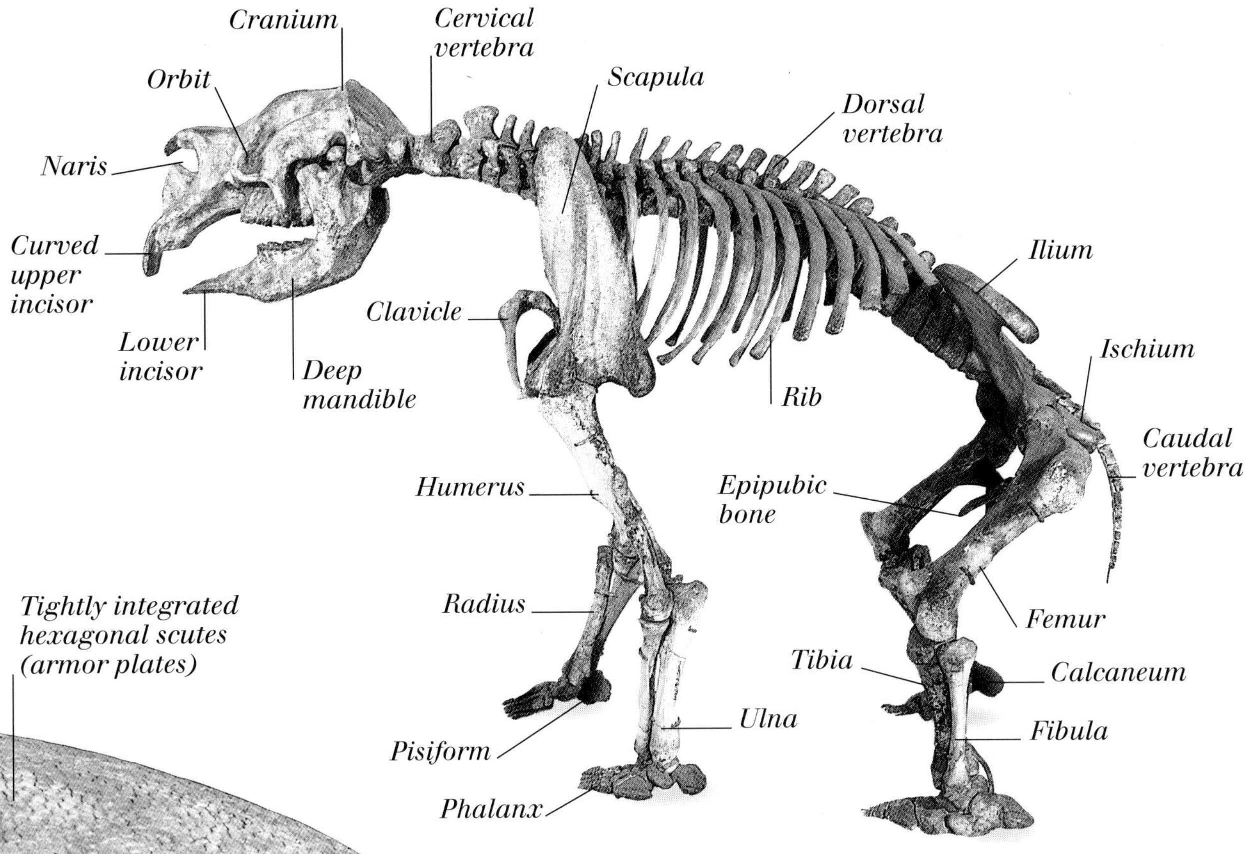

Cranium

Cervical vertebra

Orbit

Scapula

Dorsal vertebra

Naris

Curved upper incisor

Clavicle

Ilium

Lower incisor

Deep mandible

Rib

Ischium

Humerus

Epipubic bone

Caudal vertebra

Radius

Femur

Tibia

Calcaneum

Ulna

Fibula

Pisiform

Phalanx

PLEISTOCENE MARSUPIAL
(Diprotodon australis)
Length: 10 ft (3 m)

Tightly integrated hexagonal scutes (armor plates)

PLIOCENE MONOTREME
Platypus *(Ornithorhynchus* sp.)
Length: 24 in (60 cm)

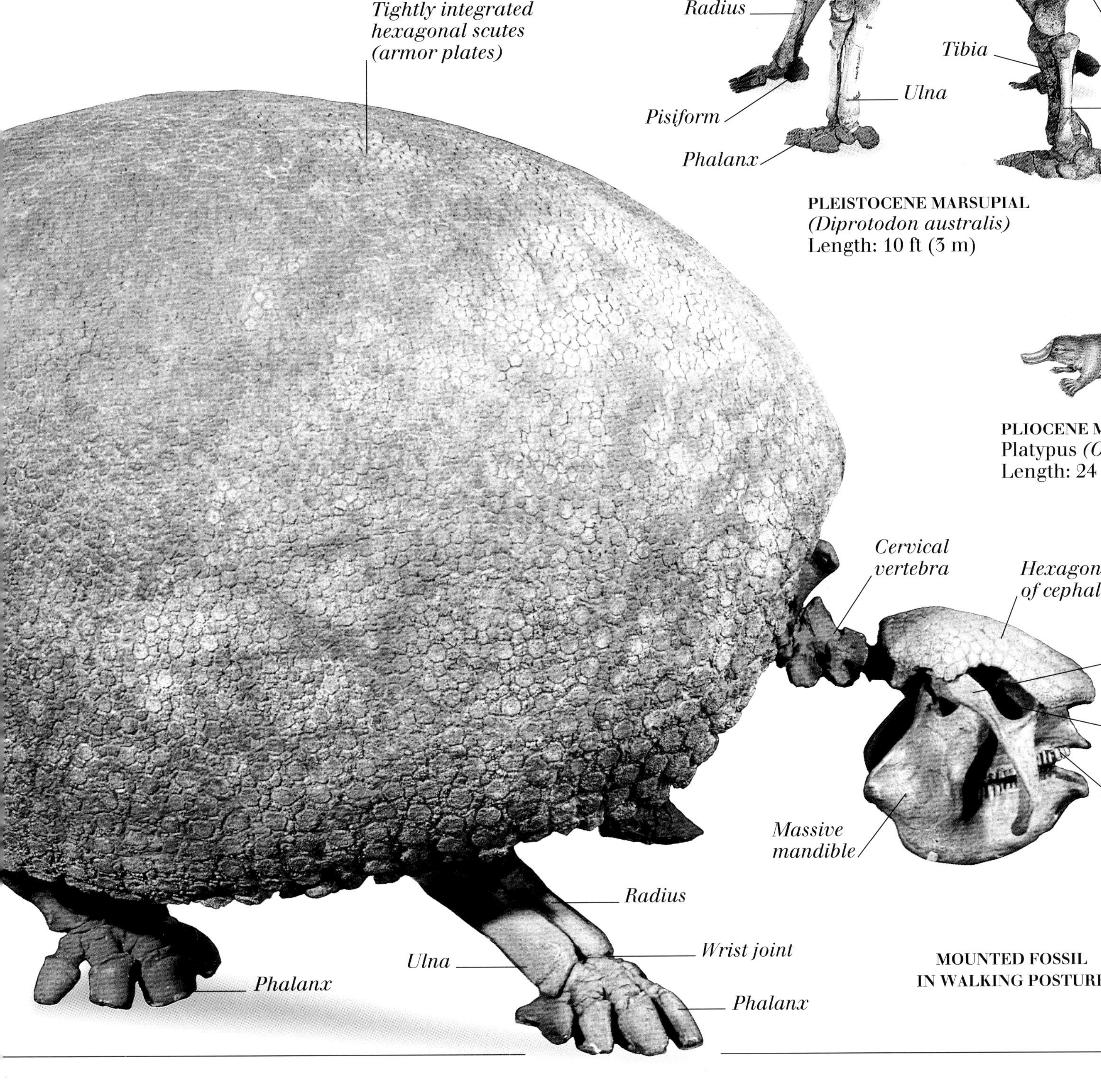

Cervical vertebra

Hexagonal scutes of cephalic shield

Zygomatic arch

Orbit

Continually growing teeth without enamel

Massive mandible

Radius

Wrist joint

Ulna

MOUNTED FOSSIL IN WALKING POSTURE

Phalanx

Phalanx

Carnivorous mammals

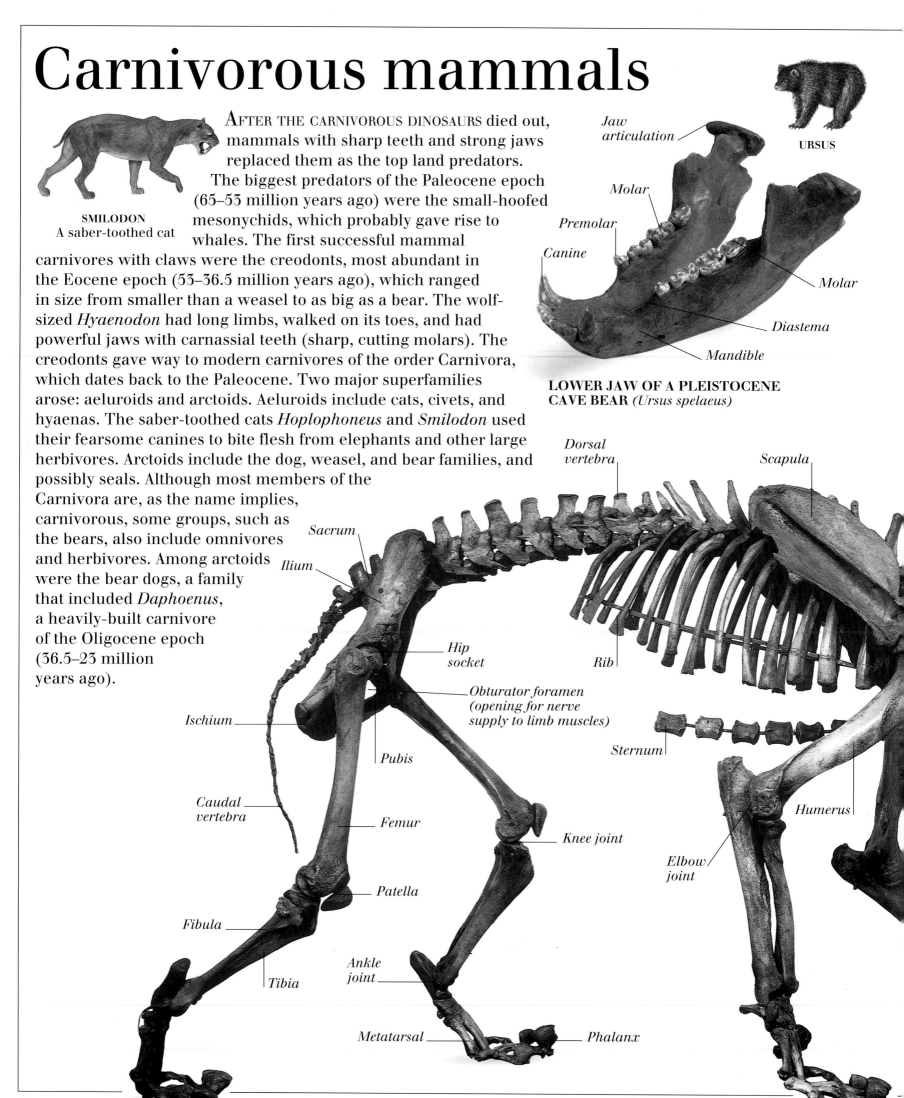

AFTER THE CARNIVOROUS DINOSAURS died out, mammals with sharp teeth and strong jaws replaced them as the top land predators. The biggest predators of the Paleocene epoch (65–53 million years ago) were the small-hoofed mesonychids, which probably gave rise to whales. The first successful mammal carnivores with claws were the creodonts, most abundant in the Eocene epoch (53–36.5 million years ago), which ranged in size from smaller than a weasel to as big as a bear. The wolf-sized *Hyaenodon* had long limbs, walked on its toes, and had powerful jaws with carnassial teeth (sharp, cutting molars). The creodonts gave way to modern carnivores of the order Carnivora, which dates back to the Paleocene. Two major superfamilies arose: aeluroids and arctoids. Aeluroids include cats, civets, and hyaenas. The saber-toothed cats *Hoplophoneus* and *Smilodon* used their fearsome canines to bite flesh from elephants and other large herbivores. Arctoids include the dog, weasel, and bear families, and possibly seals. Although most members of the Carnivora are, as the name implies, carnivorous, some groups, such as the bears, also include omnivores and herbivores. Among arctoids were the bear dogs, a family that included *Daphoenus*, a heavily-built carnivore of the Oligocene epoch (36.5–23 million years ago).

SMILODON
A saber-toothed cat

URSUS

Jaw articulation

Molar

Premolar

Canine

Molar

Diastema

Mandible

LOWER JAW OF A PLEISTOCENE CAVE BEAR (*Ursus spelaeus*)

Dorsal vertebra

Scapula

Sacrum

Ilium

Hip socket

Rib

Obturator foramen (opening for nerve supply to limb muscles)

Ischium

Sternum

Pubis

Caudal vertebra

Femur

Knee joint

Humerus

Elbow joint

Patella

Fibula

Ankle joint

Tibia

Metatarsal

Phalanx

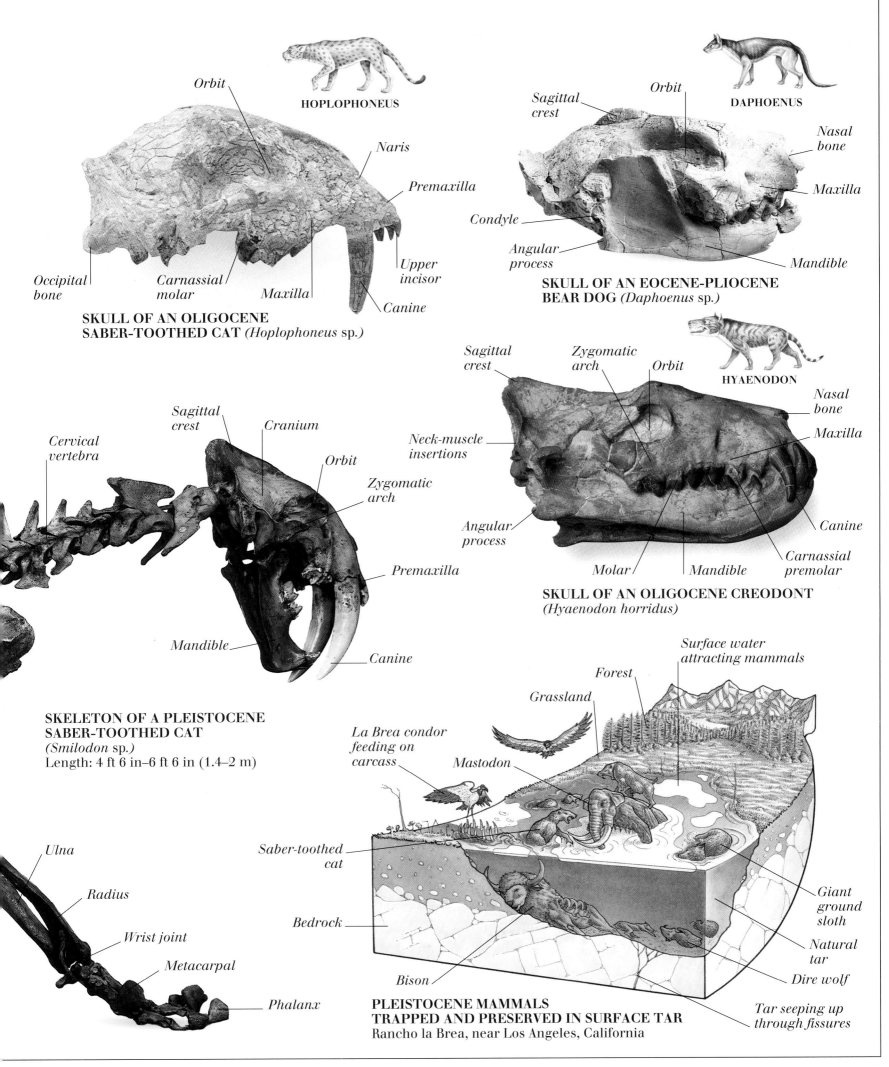

Orbit

HOPLOPHONEUS

Naris

Premaxilla

Occipital
bone

Carnassial
molar

Maxilla

Upper
incisor

Canine

**SKULL OF AN OLIGOCENE
SABER-TOOTHED CAT** (*Hoplophoneus* sp.)

Sagittal
crest

Orbit

DAPHOENUS

Nasal
bone

Maxilla

Condyle

Angular
process

Mandible

**SKULL OF AN EOCENE-PLIOCENE
BEAR DOG** (*Daphoenus* sp.)

Sagittal
crest

Zygomatic
arch

Orbit

HYAENODON

Nasal
bone

Neck-muscle
insertions

Maxilla

Angular
process

Canine

Molar

Mandible

Carnassial
premolar

SKULL OF AN OLIGOCENE CREODONT
(*Hyaenodon horridus*)

Sagittal
crest

Cranium

Cervical
vertebra

Orbit

Zygomatic
arch

Premaxilla

Mandible

Canine

**SKELETON OF A PLEISTOCENE
SABER-TOOTHED CAT**
(*Smilodon* sp.)
Length: 4 ft 6 in–6 ft 6 in (1.4–2 m)

Surface water
attracting mammals

Forest

Grassland

La Brea condor
feeding on
carcass

Mastodon

Ulna

Radius

Wrist joint

Metacarpal

Saber-toothed
cat

Bedrock

Giant
ground
sloth

Natural
tar

Phalanx

Bison

Dire wolf

Tar seeping up
through fissures

**PLEISTOCENE MAMMALS
TRAPPED AND PRESERVED IN SURFACE TAR**
Rancho la Brea, near Los Angeles, California

Hoofed mammals

THE HOOFED MAMMALS, OR UNGULATES, are herbivores derived from small, fleet-footed ancestors that ran on tiptoe to escape from predators. Ungulates developed long upper foot bones and tended to lose outer toes, sacrificing claws to gain broad, weight-bearing hooves. Two main groups arose: the perissodactyls or odd-toed ungulates, and the artiodactyls or even-toed ungulates; both appeared in the Eocene epoch (53–36.5 million years ago). An early perissodactyl was the fox-sized *Hyracotherium*, the first known horse. In the Oligocene epoch (36.5–23 million years ago), perissodactyls reached enormous sizes: *Brontotherium* was 13 ft (4 m) long, and the hornless giant rhinoceros *Paraceratherium* weighed up to 20 tons and was possibly the heaviest-ever land mammal. The 13-ft-long (4 m) woolly rhinoceros *Coelodonta* had a shaggy coat adapted for survival in the glacial phases of the Pleistocene (2 million–10,000 years ago). Artiodactyls evolved in great variety: the Oligocene mammals *Cainotherium* and *Merycoidodon* were distant relatives of camels, and the mooselike *Sivatherium* from the Pliocene (5.5–2 million years ago) was an early relative of the giraffe. The present-day bison also dates back to the Pliocene. In South America, which was an island between roughly 73 and 3 million years ago, several groups of hoofed mammals developed, including the notoungulates. The last survivor of these was the rhinoceros-sized *Toxodon*, which flourished in the Pleistocene.

EXAMPLES OF PERISSODACTYLS

COELODONTA
A Miocene-Pleistocene woolly rhinoceros
Length: 13 ft (4 m)

BRONTOTHERIUM
An Oligocene brontothere
Length: 13 ft (4 m)

PARACERATHERIUM
An Oligocene hornless rhinoceros
Length: 23 ft (7 m)

TOXODON
A Pleistocene notoungulate
Length: 10 ft (3 m)

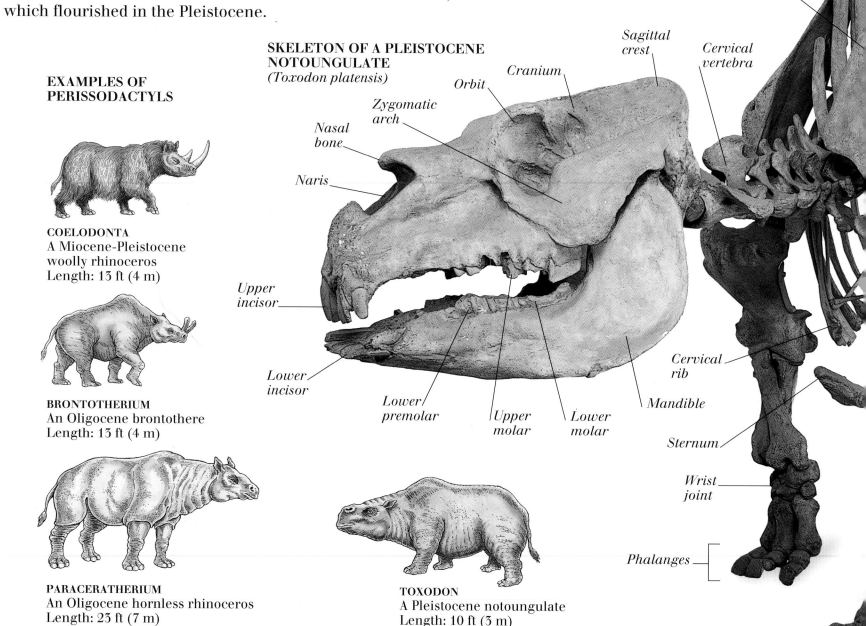

SKELETON OF A PLEISTOCENE NOTOUNGULATE
(Toxodon platensis)

Scapula

Sagittal crest

Cervical vertebra

Cranium

Orbit

Zygomatic arch

Nasal bone

Naris

Upper incisor

Lower incisor

Lower premolar

Upper molar

Lower molar

Mandible

Cervical rib

Sternum

Wrist joint

Phalanges

EXAMPLES OF ARTIODACTYLS

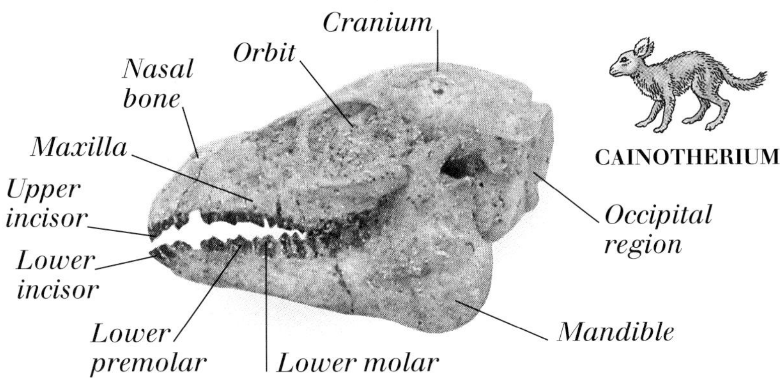

SKULL OF CAINOTHERIUM

Cranium

Orbit

Nasal bone

Maxilla

Upper incisor

Lower incisor

Lower premolar

Lower molar

Mandible

Occipital region

CAINOTHERIUM

SKULL OF CAINOTHERIUM

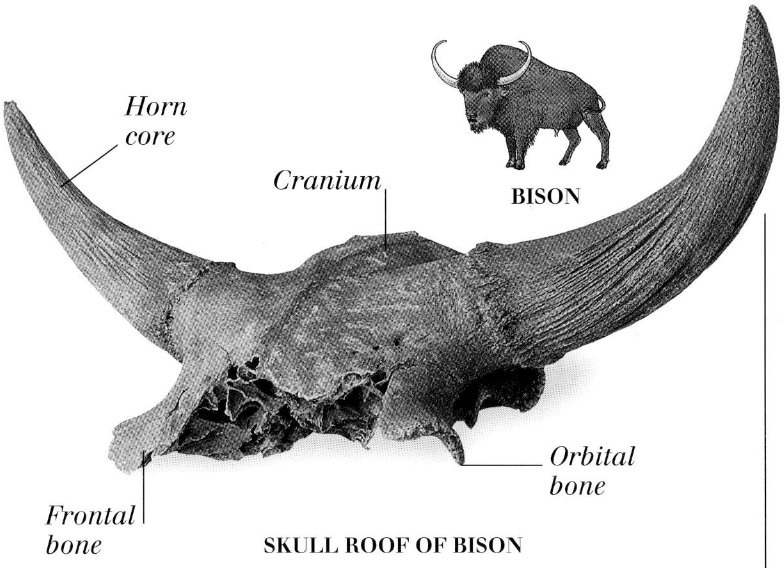

SKULL ROOF OF BISON

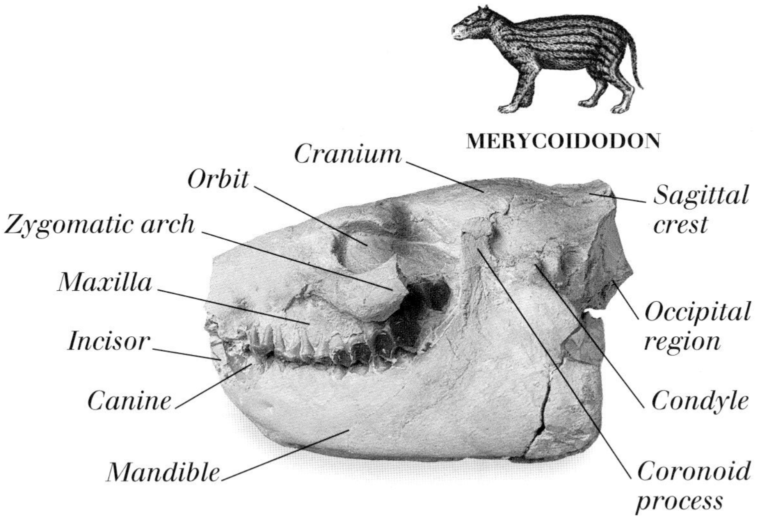

Horn core

Cranium

BISON

Orbital bone

Frontal bone

SKULL ROOF OF BISON

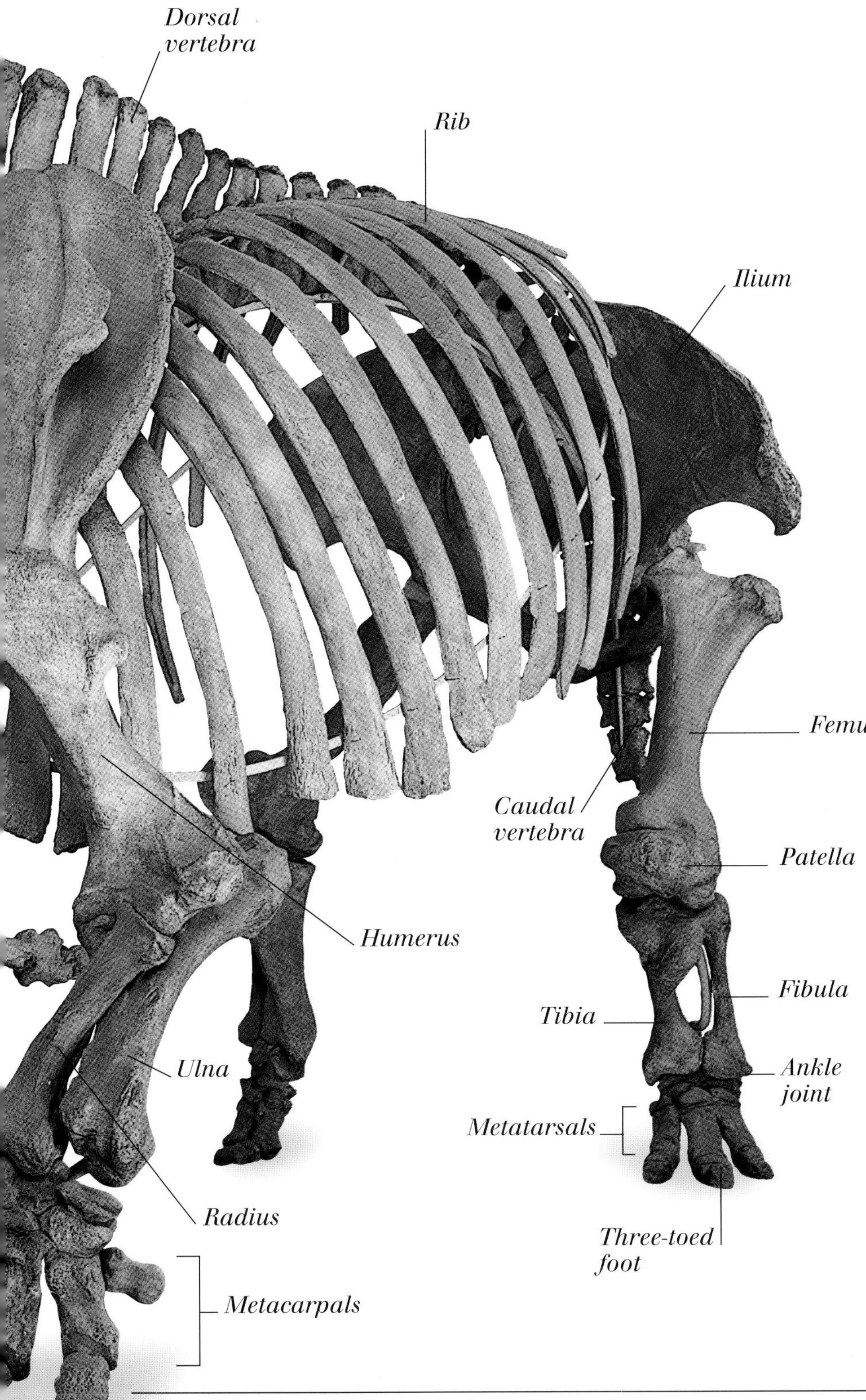

Skeleton

Dorsal vertebra

Rib

Ilium

Humerus

Caudal vertebra

Femur

Patella

Fibula

Tibia

Ankle joint

Metatarsals

Three-toed foot

Ulna

Radius

Metacarpals

SKULL OF MERYCOIDODON

MERYCOIDODON

Cranium

Orbit

Zygomatic arch

Maxilla

Incisor

Canine

Mandible

Sagittal crest

Occipital region

Condyle

Coronoid process

SKULL OF MERYCOIDODON

SKULL OF SIVATHERIUM

SIVATHERIUM

Horn core

Front ossicone

Nasal bone

Maxilla

Orbit

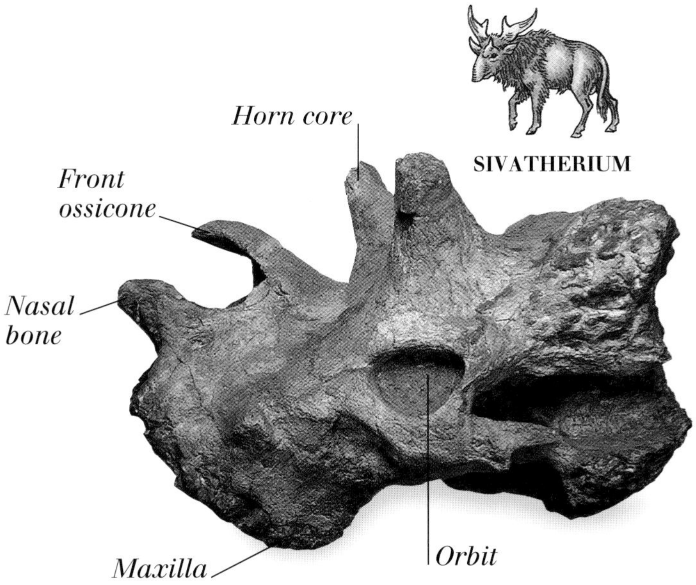

SKULL OF SIVATHERIUM

51

Elephants and their kin

THE TWO LIVING SPECIES OF ELEPHANT—African and Indian—are the only surviving representatives of the proboscideans, a group that was widespread throughout much of the Cenozoic era. One of the first proboscideans was *Moeritherium*. A herbivore from Oligocene Africa, it had small molars, rudimentary tusks, and a long upper lip that foreshadowed an elephant's fleshy trunk. Tusks developed as extensions of the incisor teeth; some of the proboscideans, notably the gomphotheres, possessed two pairs. *Phiomia*, a horse-sized Oligocene gomphothere, had a small trunk, high-crowned molars, short upper tusks, and a pair of shovel-shaped tusks in the lower jaw. The Miocene *Gomphotherium* had equally long upper and lower tusks. Among later proboscideans was the Pliocene *Stegodon*, a 23-ft-long (7 m) mammutoid with 10-ft-long (3 m) upper tusks and one to three huge molars in each jaw. The oldest known fossil elephants are about 5 million years old are found in Africa. Mammoths appeared earlier, and one of the most famous extinct elephants is the woolly mammoth, which had a thick insulating coat adapted for the extreme climatic conditions of the glacial phases of the Pleistocene epoch (2 million to 10,000 years ago). One theory for its demise is that it was hunted to extinction by early humans.

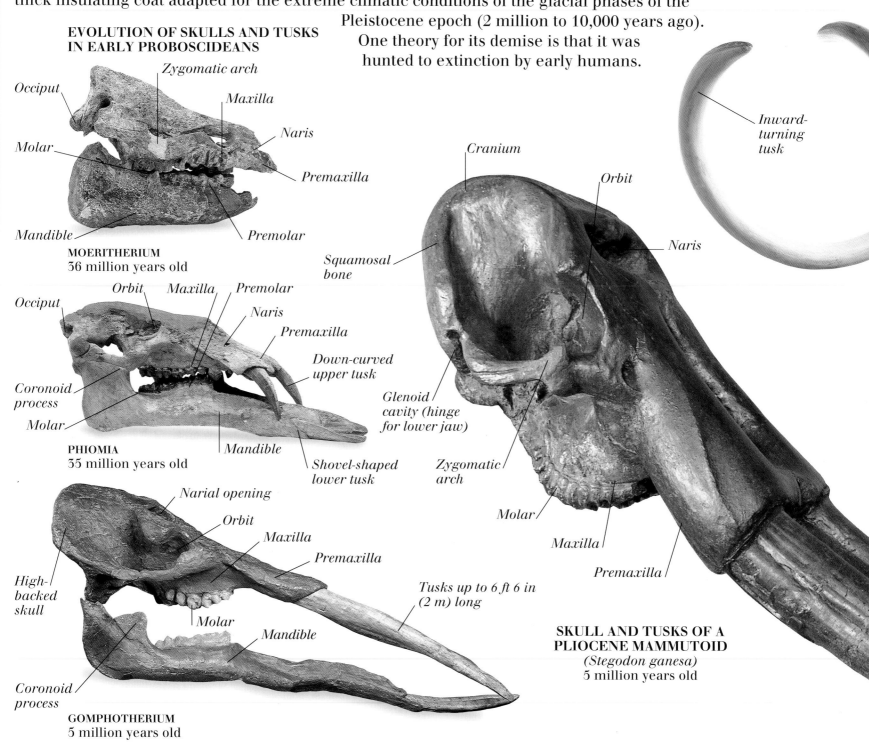

EVOLUTION OF SKULLS AND TUSKS IN EARLY PROBOSCIDEANS

Zygomatic arch
Occiput
Maxilla
Molar
Naris
Premaxilla
Mandible
Premolar

MOERITHERIUM
36 million years old

Occiput
Orbit
Maxilla
Premolar
Naris
Premaxilla
Coronoid process
Down-curved upper tusk
Molar
Mandible
Shovel-shaped lower tusk

PHIOMIA
35 million years old

Narial opening
Orbit
Maxilla
Premaxilla
High-backed skull
Molar
Mandible
Coronoid process

GOMPHOTHERIUM
5 million years old

Cranium
Orbit
Naris
Inward-turning tusk
Squamosal bone
Glenoid cavity (hinge for lower jaw)
Zygomatic arch
Molar
Maxilla
Premaxilla

Tusks up to 6 ft 6 in (2 m) long

SKULL AND TUSKS OF A PLIOCENE MAMMUTOID
(Stegodon ganesa)
5 million years old

EXAMPLES OF PROBOSCIDEANS

Pinna (ear flap)

Rump

Long, flexible lip

Short leg

Belly

MOERITHERIUM
An Oligocene moerithere
Height: 3 ft 3 in (1 m)

Domed forehead

Pinna (ear flap)

Trunk

Short tusk (upper incisor)

Tail

Shovel-shaped tusk (lower incisor)

Belly

PHIOMIA
An Oligocene gomphothere
Height: 8 ft (2.4 m)

Flat forehead

Pinna (ear flap)

Tusk (upper incisor)

Tail

Belly

LOXODONTA
Modern African elephant
Height: 13 ft (4 m)

High cranium

Eye

Small ear

Arched back

Shoulder

Rump

Thigh

Thick insulating coat

Hind leg

Thick woolly underhair

Forelimb

Lower "lip"

Belly

Ankle

Hair-covered trunk

Upper "lip"

Toenail

Heel

Foot

FEATURES OF A PLEISTOCENE MAMMUTOID
Woolly mammoth *(Mammuthus primigenius)*
Height: 13 ft (4 m)

Tusks 10 ft (3 m) long

53

Primates

HUMANS, MONKEYS, APES, AND LEMURS are primates—agile
animals originally adapted for living in trees. Apes and Old
World monkeys sprang from creatures such as *Aegyptopithecus*,
living in the Oligocene, some 36.5 million years ago.
In the Late Miocene, about 6 million years ago, early apes
gave rise to the family Hominidae, to which humans belong.
Hominids, whose earliest known genus was *Australopithecus*,
were the first primates to walk upright. The genus *Homo*
(humans) evolved in the Pliocene, by 2.5 million years ago.
Its first members (*Homo rudolfensis* and *Homo habilis*)
were shorter than modern humans, and made chipped-
stone tools. *Homo erectus* had appeared by 1.8 million
years ago and, by 500,000 years ago, gave rise to *Homo
sapiens*, whose subspecies include neanderthals and
modern humans. Neanderthals lived from 200,000
to 30,000 years ago, spanning at least two of the
Pleistocene's icy climatic phases. Modern humans
had evolved in Africa by 100,000 years ago. With their
more advanced hunting methods they colonized
much of the world, and by 30,000 years ago they
had driven the neanderthals into extinction.

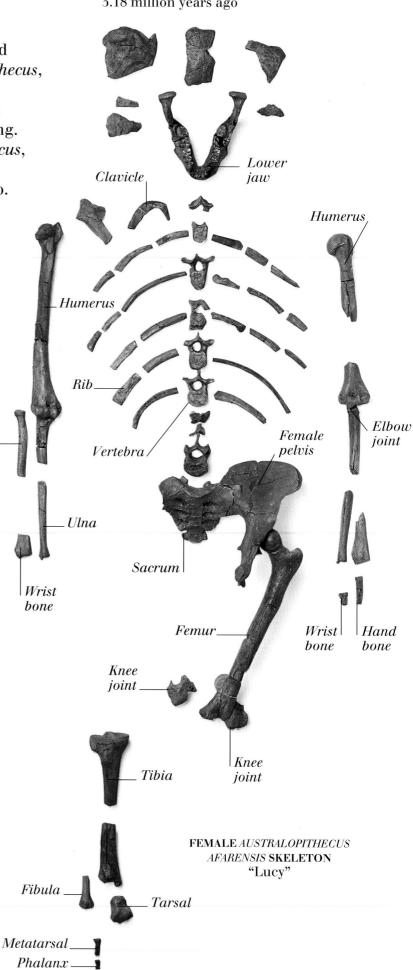

FEATURES OF A PLIOCENE HOMINID
(*Australopithecus afarensis*)
3.18 million years ago

Clavicle

Lower
jaw

Humerus

Humerus

Rib

Radius

Vertebra

Female
pelvis

Elbow
joint

Ulna

Sacrum

Wrist
bone

Femur

Wrist
bone

Hand
bone

Knee
joint

Knee
joint

Tibia

FEMALE *AUSTRALOPITHECUS*
AFARENSIS **SKELETON**
"Lucy"

Fibula

Tarsal

Metatarsal

Phalanx

RECONSTRUCTION OF
***AUSTRALOPITHECUS AFARENSIS* PAIR**
Male height: 4 ft 9 in (1.45 m)

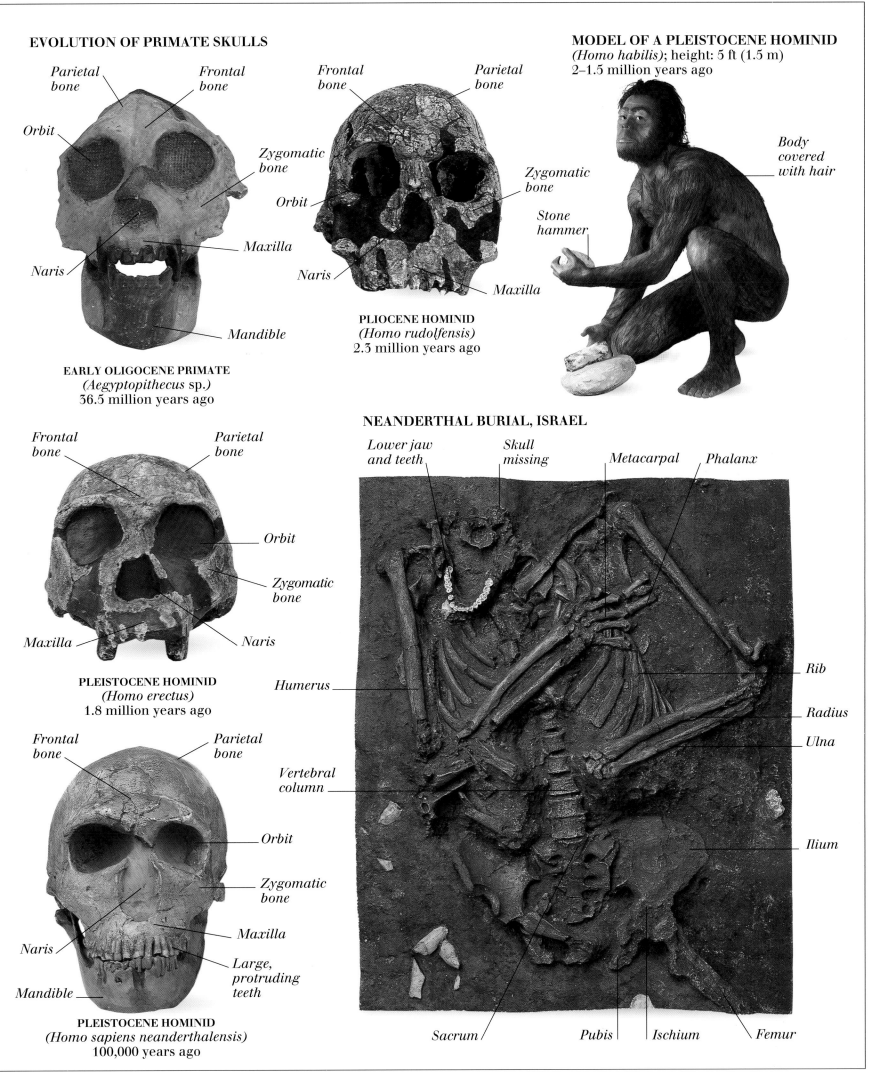

EVOLUTION OF PRIMATE SKULLS

Parietal bone

Frontal bone

Orbit

Zygomatic bone

Naris

Maxilla

Mandible

EARLY OLIGOCENE PRIMATE
(*Aegyptopithecus* sp.)
36.5 million years ago

Frontal bone

Parietal bone

Orbit

Zygomatic bone

Naris

Maxilla

PLIOCENE HOMINID
(*Homo rudolfensis*)
2.3 million years ago

MODEL OF A PLEISTOCENE HOMINID
(*Homo habilis*); height: 5 ft (1.5 m)
2–1.5 million years ago

Body covered with hair

Stone hammer

Frontal bone

Parietal bone

Orbit

Zygomatic bone

Maxilla

Naris

PLEISTOCENE HOMINID
(*Homo erectus*)
1.8 million years ago

Frontal bone

Parietal bone

Orbit

Zygomatic bone

Maxilla

Large, protruding teeth

Naris

Mandible

PLEISTOCENE HOMINID
(*Homo sapiens neanderthalensis*)
100,000 years ago

NEANDERTHAL BURIAL, ISRAEL

Lower jaw and teeth

Skull missing

Metacarpal

Phalanx

Humerus

Rib

Radius

Ulna

Vertebral column

Ilium

Sacrum

Pubis

Ischium

Femur

55

Time chart: animals

KEY

INVERTEBRATES

- SPONGES
- CORALS, ETC.
- ANNELID WORMS
- ARTHROPODS
- MOLLUSKS
- BRYOZOANS
- BRACHIOPODS
- ECHINODERMS
- HEMICHORDATES

VERTEBRATES

- CHORDATES

THE FIRST ANIMALS APPEARED in Precambrian time, evolving from animal-like members of the protist kingdom (single-celled organisms with a cell nucleus). During the Phanerozoic eon (550 million years ago to the present), the main animal groups emerged and flourished, some becoming extinct. Insects have become the most diverse group of animals today, accounting for at least three-quarters of all living species. They far outstrip the mammals, which are generally considered the dominant animal group of modern time. This chart shows a selection of the main animal groups through geological time and indicates how they are related to one another. The widths of the colored pathways broadly reflect the varying abundance of the animals in the groups. The colors of the pathways each correspond to a phylum (plural: phyla), a major unit of animal classification. Abrupt narrowings of the pathways reveal two of the most severe extinction events in the history of the animal kingdom, occurring at the end of the Permian and the Cretaceous periods. During each of these events, thousands of animal species became extinct.

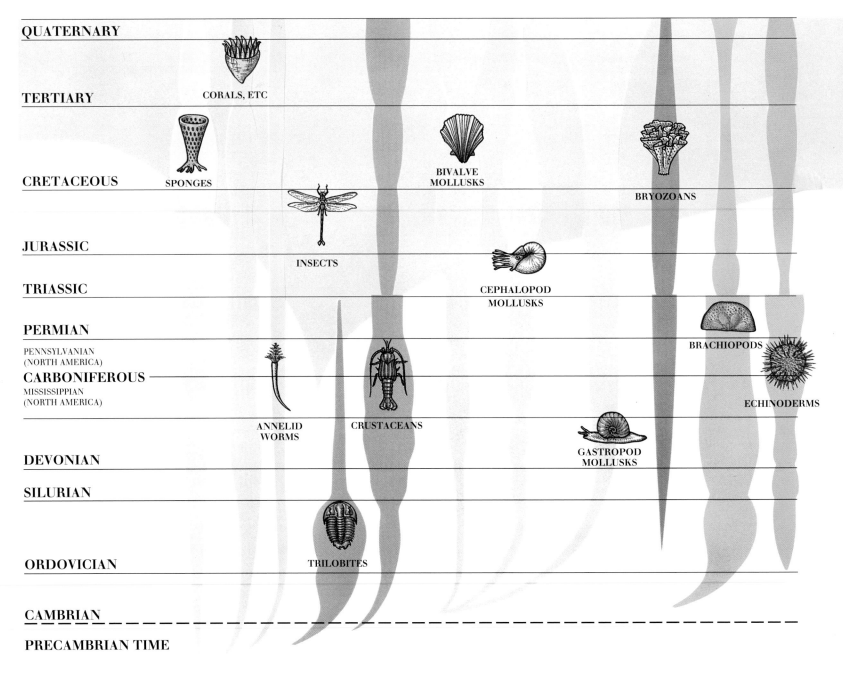

QUATERNARY

TERTIARY

CORALS, ETC

CRETACEOUS — SPONGES — BIVALVE MOLLUSKS — BRYOZOANS

JURASSIC — INSECTS

TRIASSIC — CEPHALOPOD MOLLUSKS

PERMIAN

PENNSYLVANIAN (NORTH AMERICA) — BRACHIOPODS

CARBONIFEROUS

MISSISSIPPIAN (NORTH AMERICA) — ECHINODERMS

ANNELID WORMS — CRUSTACEANS — GASTROPOD MOLLUSKS

DEVONIAN

SILURIAN

ORDOVICIAN — TRILOBITES

CAMBRIAN

PRECAMBRIAN TIME

EXAMPLES OF EXTINCT LIFE FORMS

TRILOBITE
A type of arthropod that flourished in shallow seas from the Cambrian (when it was the dominant life form) to the Permian period.

GRAPTOLITE
Sea-dwelling organisms that formed colonies, sometimes spiral in shape, and lived from the Cambrian to the Carboniferous period.

JAWLESS FISH
Apart from the 32 living species of hagfishes and lampreys, the jawless fishes died out by the end of the Devonian period.

SEA SCORPION
The sea scorpions were a group of arthropods, some as large as a human being, that died out during the Paleozoic era.

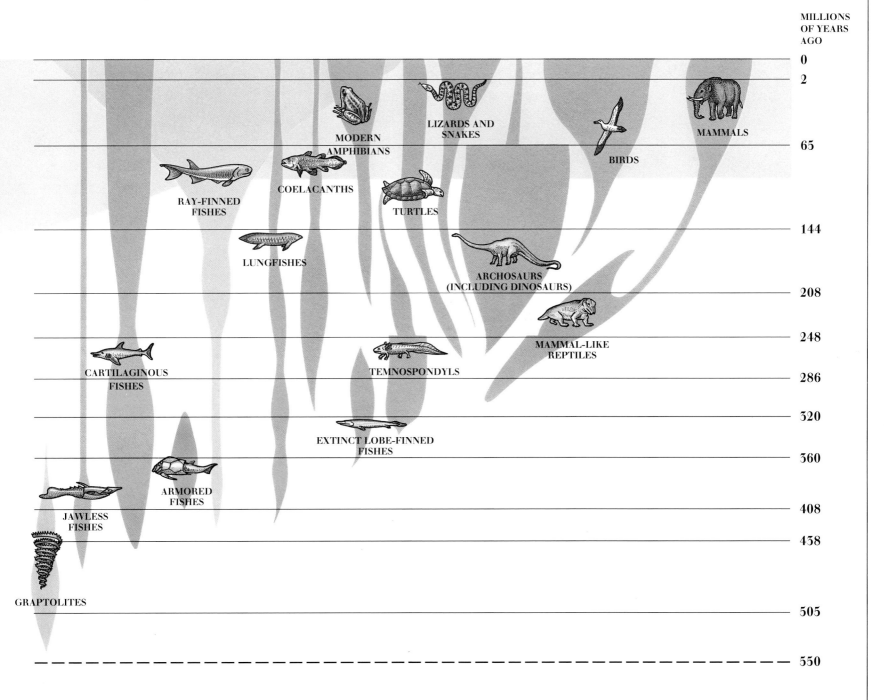

MILLIONS OF YEARS AGO

0
2

MODERN AMPHIBIANS

LIZARDS AND SNAKES

MAMMALS

65

BIRDS

RAY-FINNED FISHES

COELACANTHS

TURTLES

144

LUNGFISHES

ARCHOSAURS (INCLUDING DINOSAURS)

208

MAMMAL-LIKE REPTILES

248

CARTILAGINOUS FISHES

TEMNOSPONDYLS

286

320

EXTINCT LOBE-FINNED FISHES

360

ARMORED FISHES

408

JAWLESS FISHES

438

GRAPTOLITES

505

550

Time chart: plants

THE STORY OF THE PLANT KINGDOM begins with Precambrian algae and culminates in the present-day dominance of flowering plants, after their dramatic diversification in the middle of the Cretaceous period around 100 million years ago. This chart illustrates the changing pattern of the world's plant groups, as well as their origins and extinctions. The widths of the colored pathways reflect the prominence of each group in the world's flora. The basic unit of plant classification is the division, and in general, each color represents a division. One exception is the single color that corresponds to the algae, of which there are several divisions. The algae are not shown to scale because many authorities consider that most of them are not plants, but protists (single-celled organisms with a nucleus) or colonies of protists.

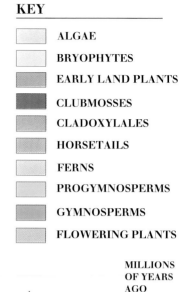

KEY

	ALGAE
	BRYOPHYTES
	EARLY LAND PLANTS
	CLUBMOSSES
	CLADOXYLALES
	HORSETAILS
	FERNS
	PROGYMNOSPERMS
	GYMNOSPERMS
	FLOWERING PLANTS

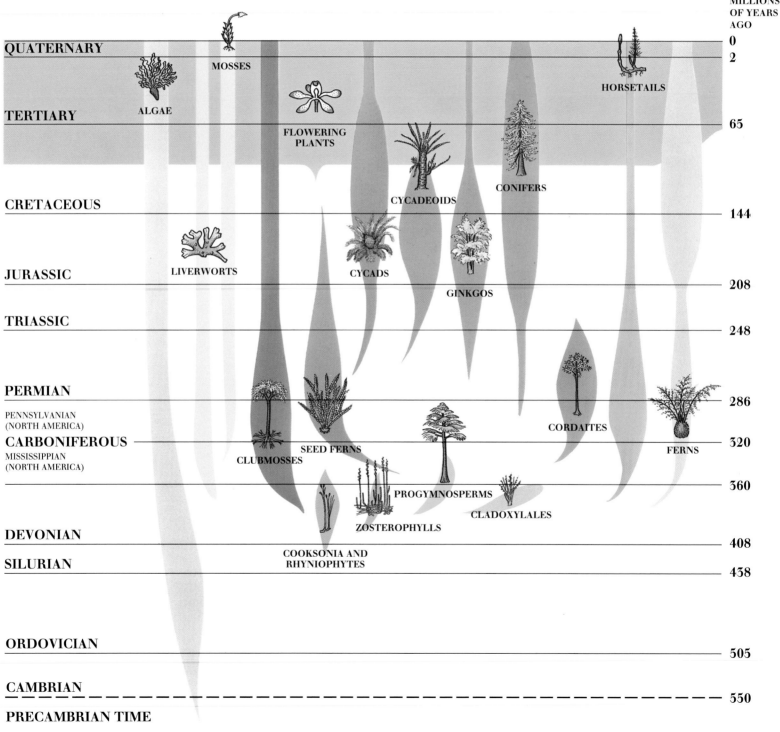

MILLIONS OF YEARS AGO

QUATERNARY — 0 — 2

MOSSES

HORSETAILS

ALGAE

TERTIARY — 65

FLOWERING PLANTS

CYCADEOIDS

CONIFERS

CRETACEOUS — 144

LIVERWORTS

CYCADS

GINKGOS

JURASSIC — 208

TRIASSIC — 248

PERMIAN — 286

PENNSYLVANIAN (NORTH AMERICA)

CORDAITES

FERNS

CARBONIFEROUS — 320

MISSISSIPPIAN (NORTH AMERICA)

SEED FERNS

CLUBMOSSES

— 360

PROGYMNOSPERMS

CLADOXYLALES

ZOSTEROPHYLLS

DEVONIAN — 408

COOKSONIA AND RHYNIOPHYTES

SILURIAN — 438

ORDOVICIAN — 505

CAMBRIAN — 550

PRECAMBRIAN TIME

Index

A

Abdomen 27
Abdominal segment 27
Acanthodians 30
Acanthostega gunnari 32
Adventitious root 16
Aegyptopithecus 14, 54–55
Aeluroids 48
Africa
    Evolution of elephant
      family 52
    Evolution of modern
      humans 52
    Position in Eocene 15
    Position in Jurassic 13
    Position in Middle
      Ordovician 11
African elephant 52, 53
Aglaophyton
    Description 16
    Time chart 58
Algae
    Ancestors of spore-bearing
      plants 16
    Evolution of 8–9
    Time chart 58
Alternate generations 16
Ammonoids 24
Amniotes
    Description 34–35
    Origin 32
Amphibians
    Description 32–33
    Rise of 10
    Time chart 57
Amplexograptus maxwelli 22
Ampulla 27
Anal fin
    Cheiracanthus 30
    Coelacanth 31
    Eusthenopteron 31
    Hoplopteryx 31
    Lamprey 29
Andrias scheuchzeri 33
Angiosperms 20
Angular bone
    Ichthyosaurus 37
    Vertebrate skulls 33
Angular process
    Cynognathus 35
    Daphoenus 49
    Hyaenodon 49
Animal kingdom 56
Ankylosaurs 42, 43
Annelid worms
    Description 22, 23
    Time chart 56
Antarctica
    Position in Eocene 15
    Position in Jurassic 13
    Position in Middle
      Ordovician 11
Anteaters, spiny 46
Anterior crural muscle
    Carnotaurus 40
    Patagopteryx 45
Anterior dorsal fin
    Coelacanth 31
    Lamprey 29

Anther 21
Antiarch 29
Antler 15
Antorbital fenestra
    Hesperornis 45
Anus 24
Aorta 28
Apatosaurus 40
Apes 54
Apical disk
    Sea urchin 26
    Starfish 27
Aptychus 24
Arabia
    Position in Jurassic 13
Archaean aeon 6, 8
Archaeopteryx lithographica
    44, 45
Archegonium 17, 19
Archosauromorphs **38–39**
Archosaurs
    Description 38–43
    Time chart 57
Arctoids 48
Armadillos 46
Armored dinosaurs 42, 43
Armored fishes 57
Arsinoitherium 15
Arthrodire 29
Arthropods
    Description **26–27**
    First appearance 10
    Time chart 56
Articular bone
    Archaeopteryx 45
    Hesperornis 45
    Osteodontornis 45
Artiodactyls 50, 51
Asia
    Position in Eocene 15
    Position in Jurassic 13
Asia, Central
    Position in Middle
      Ordovician 15
Asteroceras obtusum 24
Asterophyllites 16
Australopithecus 54
Avimimus 40
Australia
    Mammals 14
    Position in Eocene 15
    Position in Jurassic 13
    Position in Middle
      Ordovician 11
Awn 21

B

Backbone 28
Bacteria 8–9
Basal plate 27
Basilosaurus 14
Beak
    Birds 44–45
    Euoplocephalus 43
    Minmi 43
Bear dogs 48, 49
Bear family 48
Beech family 20

Belemnites 24
Belemnoteuthis antiqua 24
Belly rib
    Cryptoclidus 36
Benthosuchus 12
Berriochloa 21
Betula 14
Biped, first known 38
Birch, Miocene 14
Birds
    Description **44–45**
    First appearance 12
    Time chart 57
Bison 49, 50
Bivalves
    Description 24, 25
    Time chart 56
Bony fishes 30, 31
Bony skeletons 30
Bony-toothed birds 44, 45
Bothriolepis 28
Boxwood family 20
Brachial valve 25
Brachiopods
    Description **24–25**
    Time chart 56
Bract 20
Bract scale 18
Branchial mantle cavity
    Ammonite 24
Brontotherium 50
Brow horn core
    Arsinoitherium 15
    Triceratops 42
Brown alga 16
Bryce Canyon 6
Bryophytes
    Time chart 58
Bryozoans
    Description 22, 23
    Time chart 56
Buccal cavity
    Cephalaspid 28
Bulb plants 20
Burgess Shale, Canada 22
Butterfly shell 25
Bythotrephis gracilis 16

C

Cainotherium 50, 51
Calcaneum
    Diprotodon 47
Cambrian period
    Early invertebrates 22
    In geological timescale 6
    In Paleozoic era 10
    Mollusks and brachiopods
      24
Camels 50
Cancellothyris platys 25
Canda foliifera 23
Canine tooth
    Aegyptopithecus 14
    Cynognathus 35
    Dimetrodon 11
    Hyaenodon 49
    Merycoidodon 51
    Smilodon 49
    Ursus spelaeus 48
Carapace
    Glyptodon 47
    Shrimp 27
Carbon dioxide 8
Carbonaceous film 16

Carboniferous period
    Early invertebrates 22
    Early reptiles 34
    Early spore-bearing
      plants 16
    First diapsid reptiles 36
    Gymnosperms 18
    In geological timescale 6–7
    In Paleozoic era 10
    Primitive fishes 28
Carnassial premolar
    Hoplophoneus 49
    Hyaenodon 49
Carnassial teeth 48
Carnivora 48
Carnivores
    Cenozoic key events 15
    Mammals 48
Carnivorous mammals **48–49**
Carnivorous therapsid
    reptiles 34–35
Carnotaurus sastrei 41
Carpal 36
Carpoids 26
Carpopenaeus callirostris 27
Cartilaginous fishes
    Description 30
    Time chart 57
Cat family 48
Caudal fin
    Eusthenopteron 31
    Lamprey 29
    Panderichthys 31
Caudal fin ray
    Coelacanth 31
    Hoplopteryx 31
Caudal musculature
    Carnotaurus 40
Caudal vertebra
    Carnotaurus 40
    Compsognathus 41
    Diprotodon 47
    Euoplocephalus 43
    Euparkeria 38
    Neusticosaurus 37
    Protoceratops 42
    Scaphonyx 39
    Smilodon 48
    Cryptoclidus 36
Cave bear 48
Cedar, Japanese 18
Cenozoic era
    Description **14–15**
    In geological timescale 7
    Key events 14–15
    Mammals 48–55
Central Asia, position in
    Middle Ordovician 11
Cephalaspids 28
Cephalaspis 28
Cephalic shield
    Glyptodon 47
    Graptolite 22
Cephalochordates 28
Cephalon 27
Cephalopods
    Description 24
    Time chart 56
Ceratopsians 42
Ceratozamia 19
Cervical musculature
    Carnotaurus 41
    Euoplocephalus 43
    Euparkeria 39
Cervical rib 50

Cervical vertebra
    Archaeopteryx 44
    Compsognathus 41
    Cryptoclidus 36
    Diprotodon 47
    Glyptodon 47
    Neusticosaurus 37
    Patagopteryx 44
    Scaphonyx 39
    Smilodon 49
    Toxodon 50
    Sinokannemeyeria 34
Cheiracanthus 30
Chelicerates 26
Chevron
    Cryptoclidus 36
    Eryops 33
    Euoplocephalus 43
    Protoceratops 42
China, position in Middle
    Ordovician 11
Chitons 24, 25
Chloroplast 9
Chondrichthyes 30
Chordates 56
Cilia 26
Cilium 26
Cladoxylales 58
Clavicle 47
Claw
    Archaeopteryx 44
    Euparkeria 39
    Glyptodon 46
    Patagopteryx 45
    Pterodactylus 38
Cloaca
    Carnotaurus 40
    Euoplocephalus 43
    Patagopteryx 45
Clubmosses
    Description 16, 17
    Time chart 58
Clypeaster 26
Cnidarians 22, 23
Coal-forming swamps 16
Coelacanths
    Description 31
    Time chart 57
Coelodonta 50
Coleopleuris
    paucituberculatus 26
Collenia 9
Colorado River 7, 15
Columella 23
Columnal 27
Complex brain 28
Compsognathus longipes
    40, 41
Condor 49
Condyle
    Daphoenus 49
    Merycoidodon 51
Conifer pollen tube 18
Conifers
    Gymnosperms 18
    In Mesozoic era 12
    Time chart 58
Continents, formation of 8
Continually growing teeth:
    Fishes 30
    Glyptodon 47
Cooksonia
    In Paleozoic era 10
    Spore-bearing plants 16
    Time chart 58

Coracoid
  Carnotaurus 41
  Euoplocephalus 43
  Euparkeria 39
Coral reefs 10
Corals
  Description 22, 23
  Time chart 56
Cordaites 58
Coronoid process
  Aegyptopithecus 14
  Cynognathus 35
  Gomphotherium 52
  Phiomia 52
Corpus
  Pollen grain 19
Cothurnocystis eliziae 26
Couperites mauldinensis 21
Crabs 26
Cranium
  Aegyptopithecus 14
  Archaeopteryx 44
  Bison 51
  Cainotherium 51
  Cynognathus 35
  Dimetrodon 11
  Diprotodon 47
  Eryops 32
  Mammuthus primigenius 53
  Merycoidodon 51
  Neusticosaurus 37
  Phorusrhacos 45
  Sinokannemeyeria 34
  Smilodon 49
  Stegoceras 42
  Stegodon 52
  Toxodon 50
Creodonts 48
Cretaceous period
  Amphibians 32
  Archosaurs 38
  Flowering plants 20
  In geological timescale 6–7
  In Mesozoic era 12
  Ornithischian dinosaurs 44
  Saurischian dinosaurs 40
Cretaceous/Tertiary
  boundary 6
Crinoids 26, 27
Crocodilians
  Archosaurs 38, 39
  Mesozoic era 12
Crown
  Sea lily 27
Crustaceans
  Description 26, 27
  Time chart 56
Cryptoclidus eurymerus 36
Cryptomeria japonica 18
Ctenidium 25
Cusps
  Mammal teeth 46
Cyamodus 37
Cyatheacidites annulata 17
Cycadeoids
  Time chart 58
Cycads
  Life cycle 18, 19
  Modern 12, 18, 19
  Time chart 58
  Triassic 13
Cycas revoluta 12, 13
Cyclothyris difformis 25
Cynognathus crateronotus 35
Cytoplasm 9

D

Dacrydium pollen 19
Daisy group 21
Daphoenus 48, 49
Deinosuchus 38, 39
Dentary bone
  Archaeopteryx 45
  Hesperornis 45
  Hoplopteryx 31
  Ichthyosaurus 37
  Osteodontornis 45
  Reptilian skulls 35
  Sinokannemeyeria 34
  Vertebrate skulls 33
Dermal armor
  Glyptodon 46
Desertification 10
Devonian period
  Amphibians 32
  Echinoderms 26
  Gymnosperms 18
  In geological timescale 7
  In Paleozoic era 10
  Placoderms 28, 29
  Spore-bearing plants 16
Diapsid reptiles
  Archosauromorphs 38–39
  Definition 34, 35
  Marine 36–37
Diapsid skull 35
Diastema
  Ursus spelaeus 48
Dicotyledons 20
Dicroidium 18
Didelphidae 46
Didelphis albiventris 46, 47
Didymaspis 28
Digital extensor muscle
  Euoplocephalus 43
Digits
  Early tetrapods 32, 33
Dimerocrinites icosidactylus 27
Dimetrodon loomisi 11
Dinictis 15
Dinosaurs
  Archosauromorphs 38
  Description **40–43**
  Extinction 12, 13
  First appearance 12, 13
  Ornithischian **40–41**
  Saurischian **42–43**
  Time chart 57
Diplocaulus magnicornis 32
Diprotodon australis 46, 47
Dire wolf 49
Dissepiment
  Coral skeleton 23
Diversification
  Flowering plants 20, 58
Division
  Plant classification 58
Dog family 48
Dolphinlike reptiles 36
Dorsal aorta 28
Dorsal fin
  Cheiracanthus 30
Dorsal fin ray
  Hoplopteryx 31
Dorsal vertebra
  Archaeopteryx 44
  Carnotaurus 41
  Compsognathus 41
  Cryptoclidus 36
  Diprotodon 47

Edaphosaurus 35
  Glyptodon 47
  Neusticosaurus 37
  Patagopteryx 45
  Protoceratops 42
  Pterodactylus 38
  Scaphonyx 39
  Sinokannemeyeria 35
  Smilodon 48
  Toxodon 51
Double fertilization 20
Dunkleosteus 28, 29

E

Ear
  Bivalve shell 25
Ear flap
  Proboscideans 53
Early humans 52
Early invertebrates **22–23**
Early mammals **46–47**
Early reptiles **34–35**
Early tetrapods
  Amphibians **32–33**
  Amniotes **34–35**
Earth, formation of 8
Earth history 6–9
Echinoderms
  Description **26–27**
  Time chart 56
Ecphora quadricostata 14
Edaphosaurus 34, 35
Edentates 46
Ediacara fossils 8, 9
Egg-laying mammals 46
Eggs
  Amniotes 34
  Cycads 19
  Flowering plants 20
  Gymnosperms 18
Elater
  Horsetail spore 16
Elbow
  Pterodactylus 38
  Eryops 32
Elephants and their kin
  52–53
Elytron 27
Embryo
  Clubmoss 17
  Cycad 19
  Flowering plant 21
Endosperm
  Cycad 19
  Flowering plant 21
Endosperm nucleus 21
Eocene
  In Cenozoic era 14
  In geological timescale 7
  Mammals 48–51
Eons
  Geological timescale 6–7
  Precambrian time 8–9
Epipubic bone
  Diprotodon 47
Epitheca 23
Epochs
  Geological timescale 6–7
  Cenozoic era 14–15
Equatorial view
  Pollen grain 21
Equisetum giganteum 16
Equisetum spore 16
Eras 6–7

Eryops megacephalus 32
Erythrosuchus 38
Esophagus 28
Estonioceras 10
Eukaryotes
  Description 8–9
  First appearance 6
Euoplocephalus tutus 42–43
Eupantothere 47
Euparkeria capensis 38–39
Europe
  Position in Eocene 15
  Position in Jurassic 13
  Position in Middle
  Ordovician 11
Eusthenopteron 30, 31
Even-toed ungulates 50, 51
Evolutionary explosion 22
Exine
  Pollen grain 18
Extinction events 56
Eye ring
  Patagopteryx 44

F

Feathers
  Archaeopteryx 44
Feather stars 26
Femoral muscle
  Patagopteryx 45
Femur
  Archaeopteryx 44
  Arsinoitherium 15
  Australopithecus 54
  Carnotaurus 41
  Compsognathus 41
  Cryptoclidus 36
  Diprotodon 47
  Eryops 32
  Euoplocephalus 43
  Euparkeria 38
  Glyptodon 46
  Neanderthal 55
  Patagopteryx 45
  Pterodactylus 38
  Scaphonyx 39
  Sinokannemeyeria 35
  Smilodon 48
  Tyrannosaurus 40
Fenestella plebeia 23
Fenestra
  Cryptoclidus 36
  Early reptile skulls 35
Fern spores 17
Ferns
  Description 16, 17
  Time chart 58
Fibula
  Arsinoitherium 15
  Australopithecus 54
  Carnotaurus 40
  Compsognathus 41
  Diprotodon 47
  Eryops 33
  Euoplocephalus 43
  Euparkeria 38
  Lobe-finned fish 31
  Neusticosaurus 37
  Ray-finned fish 31
  Sinokannemeyeria 35
  Smilodon 48
  Tyrannosaurus 40
Filament
  Flowering plant 21

Fins
  Amphibians 32–33
  Modern fishes 30–31
  Primitive fishes 28–29
Fishes
  Armored 28, 29
  Bony 30, 31
  Earliest known 28
  Lobe-finned 30, 31
  Jawless 28
  Modern 30, 31
Flagellum 9
Fleshy-finned fishes 30
Flippers of marine reptiles 36
Flowering plants
  Description **20–21**
  Mesozoic era 12
  Seed production 21
  Time chart 58
Foot bones
  Lissamphibian 33
  Neusticosaurus 37
Foramen
  Brachiopod shell 25
  Cephalaspid skull 28
  Smilodon 48
Forests, earliest 10
Frogs 32
Frontal bone
  Aegyptopithecus 55
  Archaeopteryx 45
  Bison 51
  Hesperornis 45
  Homo erectus 55
  Homo rudolfensis 55
  Hoplopteryx 31
  Ichthyosaurus 37
  Neanderthal 55
  Osteodontornis 45
  Phorusrhacos 45
  Reptilian skulls 35
  Vertebrate skulls 33

G

Gametes
  Plants 16–21
Gametophyte 16, 17
Gastrocnemius muscle 40
Gastropods
  Description 24, 25
  Time chart 56
Genal spine 27
Genital pore 26
Geological periods **6–7**
Geological timescale **6–7**
Giant ground sloth 49
Gill
  Ammonite 24
  Hoplopteryx 31
Gill chamber 28
Gill cover 33
Gill opening 29
Gill slit 33
Ginkgo
  Evolution 18
  Pollen 18
  Time chart 58
Giraffe 50
Girdle
  Chiton 25
Gizzard
  Carnotaurus 41
  Euoplocephalus 43
  Patagopteryx 45

Glabella 27
Glabellar furrow 27
Glacial phases
    In Cenozoic era 15
    Mammal groups 50–54
Glass sponge 23
Glenoid cavity 52
Glyptodon reticulatus 46–47
Gomphotheres 52, 53
Gomphotherium 52
Gonad 26
Gondwanaland 9
Grand Canyon 15
Grand Canyon region 6–7
Graptolites
    Description 22
    Time chart 57
Grass family 21
Grass husks 21
Grasses 20
Grassland
    In Cenozoic era 14, 15
    Flowering plants 20
Grazing mammals 14
Greenland 8, 11
Gristly skeletons 30
Ground sloth 49
Gubbio, Italy 6
Gymnosperms
    Description **18–19**
    Time chart 58

H

Hadrosaurs 42, 43
Hagfishes
    Evolution 28
    Time chart 57
Hallucigenia 22
Hallux
    Archaeopteryx 44
    Carnotaurus 41
    Euparkeria 38, 39
Hand bones
    Lissamphibian 33
    Neusticosaurus 37
Hazel family 20
Head crest 42, 43
Head horn 43
Head shield 28, 29
Heart
    Carnotaurus 41
    Patagopteryx 45
Helicoprion bessonowi 11
Heliobatis radians 30
Hemichordates 56
Herbivorous dinosaurs
    42–43
Herbivorous reptiles 34
Hesperornis 44, 45
Heterosporous clubmoss 16,
    17
Hexagonocaulon minutum 16
Himalayas, formation of 14
Hinge line 25
Hip girdle
    Dinosaur types 40, 41
    Tyrannosaurus 40
Hip joint
    Archaeopteryx 44
Hip socket
    Smilodon 48
Holocene epoch
    In Cenozoic era 14, 15
    In geological timescale 7

Hominidae 54
Hominids 54, 55
Homo 54
Homo erectus 54, 55
Homo habilis 54, 55
Homo rudolfensis 54, 55
Homo sapiens 54, 55
*Homo sapiens
    neanderthalensis* 55
Homo sapiens sapiens 15, 54
Hoofed mammals **50–51**
Hoplophoneus 48, 49
Hoplopteryx lewesiensis
    30, 31
Horn core
    Bison 51
    Sivatherium 51
    Triceratops 42
Horn
    Carnotaurus 41
Hornless giant rhinoceros 50
Horses 14, 50
Horseshoe crabs 26
Horsetails
    Description 16
    Time chart 58
Humans **54–55**
Humerus
    Archaeopteryx 44
    Australopithecus 54
    Carnotaurus 41
    Compsognathus 41
    Cryptoclidus 36
    Diprotodon 47
    Eryops 52
    Euoplocephalus 43
    Euparkeria 39
    Glyptodon 46
    Patagopteryx 44
    Pterodactylus 38
    Scaphonyx 39
    Smilodon 48
Hyaenodon horridus 48, 49
Hydrophilus 27
Hyponome 24
Hypural 31

I

Hyracotherium 14, 50
Ichthyornis 44
Ichthyosaurs 12, 13, 36
Ichthyosaurus communis 37
Ichthyosaurus megacephalus
    13
Icy phases of the Pleistocene
    Cenozoic era 14
    Elephants 52
    Hoofed mammals 50
    Primates 54
Iliofibularis muscle
    Euparkeria 38
Iliotibial muscle
    Euoplocephalus 43
Ilium
    Archaeopteryx 44
    Carnotaurus 40
    Cryptoclidus 36
    Diprotodon 47
    Euoplocephalus 43
    Glyptodon 46
    Minmi 43
    Neanderthal 55
    Ornithischian dinosaur 41
    Patagopteryx 45

Saurischian dinosaur 41
Sinokannemeyeria 35
Smilodon 48
Toxodon 51
Tyrannosaurus 40
Incisor
    Cainotherium 51
    Diprotodon 47
    Hoplophoneus 49
    Merycoidodon 51
    Toxodon 50
India
    Position in Eocene 15
    Position in Jurassic 13
    Position in Middle
        Ordovician 11
Indian elephants 52
Infratemporal fenestra
    Cynognathus 35
    Dimetrodon 11
    Parasaurolophus 43
    Psittacosaurus 42
    Pterodactylus 38
    Sinokannemeyeria 34
    Triceratops 42
Insects
    Description 26, 27
    Time chart 56
Integument 19
Invertebrates
    Description **22–27**
    Time chart 56
Ischium
    Archaeopteryx 44
    Carnotaurus 40
    Composognathus 41
    Cryptoclidus 36
    Diprotodon 47
    Euoplocephalus 43
    Glyptodon 46
    Neanderthal 55
    Ornithischian dinosaur 41
    Protoceratops 42
    Saurischian dinosaur 41
    Sinokannemeyeria 35
    Smilodon 48
    Toxodon 51
    Tyrannosaurus 40

J

Japanese cedar 18
Jaw articulation
    Benthosuchus 12
    Ursus spelaeus 48
Jawless fishes
    Description 28
    Time chart 57
Jugal bone
    Cynognathus 35
    Psittacosaurus 42
Jugal plate
    Aegyptopithecus 14
Jurassic period
    Early birds 44
    In geological timescale 6–7
    In Paleozoic era 12, 13
    Marine reptiles 36
    Synapsid reptiles 34

K

Kidney 39
Kieraspis 28
Kingdoms 8

L

La Brea condor 49
La Brea tar pit 49
Lacrimal bone
    Hopolopteryx 31
    Reptilian skulls 35
Lampreys
    Evolution 28, 29
    Time chart 57
Lampshell brachiopod 25
Lancelet 28
Land plants
    Palaeozoic era 10
    Spore-bearing plants 16
    Time chart 58
Landmasses
    Early movement 10
    Eocene positions 15
    Jurassic positions 13
    Middle Ordovician
        positions 11
Lappet
    Feather star 26
Large intestine
    Carnotaurus 41
    Euoplocephalus 43
    Patagopteryx 45
Lateral caudal musculature
    Euoplocephalus 43
Laurel family 20, 21
Leaf scale
    Cycas revoluta 12
Lemma
    Grass husk 21
Lemurs 54
Lepidodendron
    Bark 11
    Whole tree 17
Lepidotrichia 31
Ligament pit
    Bivalve 25
Lily family 20
Limbs, evolution of 32
Lissamphibians 32, 33
Liver
    Carnotaurus 41
    Euoplocephalus 43
    Euparkeria 39
Liverworts 16, 58
Lizards 57
Lobe
    Trilobite 27
Lobe-finned fishes
    Description 30
    In Palaeozoic era 10
    Time chart 57
Locule
    Flowering plant 21
Lophophore 22
Lucy 54
Lung
    Carnotaurus 41
    Euoplocephalus 43
    Euparkeria 39
    Patagopteryx 45
Lungfishes 57

M

Magnolias 20
Maidenhair tree 18
Male gamete
    Cycad 19
    Flowering plant 21

Mammal-like reptiles
    Description **34–35**
    Time chart 57
Mammals
    Descriptions **46–55**
    Cenozoic era 14–15
    Mesozoic era 12, 13
    Time chart 56, 57
Mammutoids 52
Mandible
    Aegyptopithecus 55
    Cainotherium 51
    Cynognathus 35
    Daphoenus 49
    Diprotodon 47
    Dunkleosteus 29
    Glyptodon 47
    Gomphotherium 52
    Hyaenodon 49
    Merycoidodon 51
    Moeritherium 52
    Neanderthal 55
    Osteodontornis 45
    Parasaurolophus 43
    Patagopteryx 44
    Phiomia 52
    Psittacosaurus 42
    Pterodactylus 38
    Smilodon 49
    Stegoceras 42
    Toxodon 50
    Triceratops 42
    Ursus spelaeus 48
Mandibular nerve 28
Maniraptorans 44
Mantle 24
Marginocephalians 42, 43
Marine invertebrates **26–27**
Marine reptiles
    Description **36–37**
    Mesozoic era 12, 13
Marsupials 46
Mass extinction events
    Mesozoic 12
    Paleozoic 10, 11
    Time chart 56
Mastodon 49
Matonia braunii 17
Matonia pectinata 17
Mauldinia mirabilis 20
Mawsonites 6, 8
Maxilla
    Aegyptopithecus 55
    Archaeopteryx 45
    Cainotherium 51
    Cynognathus 35
    Daphoenus 49
    Dimetrodon 11
    Gomphotherium 52
    Hesperornis 45
    Homo erectus 55
    Homo rudolfensis 55
    Hoplophoneus 49
    Hyaenodon 49
    Ichthyosaurus 37
    Merycoidodon 51
    Moeritherium 52
    Neanderthal 55
    Osteodontornis 45
    Phiomia 52
    Phorusrhacus 45
    Sivatherium 51
    Stegoceras 42
    Stegodon 52
    Vertebrate skulls 53

Median dorsal plate 29
Median fin 28
Megaloceros 15
Megasporangium 17
Megaspore 16, 17
Megatherium americanum 46, 47
Merycoidodon 50, 51
Mesonychids 48
Mesozoic era
    Archosaurs 38
    Description **12–13**
    In geological timescale 7
    Key events 12–13
    Marine reptiles 36
Mesozoic seascape 36
Metacarpal
    Archaeopteryx 44
    Cryptoclidus 37
    Eryops 32
    Euoplocephalus 43
    Glyptodon 46
    Neanderthal 55
    Scaphonyx 39
    Sinokannemeyeria 34
Metatarsal
    Archaeopteryx 44
    Australopithecus 54
    Carnotaurus 40
    Composognathus 41
    Eryops 33
    Euoplocephalus 43
    Euparkeria 38
    Glyptodon 46
    Pterodactylus 38
    Scaphonyx 39
    Smilodon 48
Microsporangium 17, 18
Microspore 16, 17
Miniplanets, collision with
    Earth 8
Minmi paravertebra 42, 43
Miocene epoch
    Birds 44
    Grasses 20, 21
    Hominids 54
    In Cenozoic era 14, 15
    In geological timescale 7
Mississippian period 7
Mitochondrion 9
Modern carnivores 15
Modern fishes **30–31**
Modern humans
    Cenozoic era 15
    Evolution 54
Modern reptiles 36
Moeritherium 52, 53
Molar
    Cainotherium 51
    Cynognathus 35
    Gomphotherium 52
    Moeritherium 52
    Phiomia 52
    Stegodon 52
    Toxodon 50
    Ursus spelaeus 48
Mollusks
    Description **24–24**
    Evolutionary explosion 10
    Time chart 56
Monkeys 54
Monocotyledons 20
Monograptus 23
Monotremes 46, 47
Moose 50

Mosasaurs 36
Mosses 16
Mucrospirifer mucronata 25
Multicellular organisms
    Evolution 10
    First appearance 6
Multicusped teeth 46

N

Narial opening
    Archaeopteryx 45
    Gomphotherium 52
    Hesperornis 45
Naris
    Aegyptopithecus 14, 55
    Arsinoitherium 15
    Benthosuchus 12
    Cryptoclidus 37
    Cynognathus 35
    Dimetrodon 11
    Diplocaulus 32
    Diprotodon 47
    Eryops 32
    Homo erectus 55
    Homo rudolfensis 55
    Hoplophoneus 49
    Megaloceros 14
    Moeritherium 52
    Neanderthal 55
    Parasaurolophus 43
    Phorusrhacus 45
    Psittacosaurus 42
    Sinokannemeyeria 34
    Stegodon 52
    Toxodon 50
    Triceratops 42
Nasal bone
    Cainotherium 51
    Cynognathus 35
    Daphoenus 49
    Hyaenodon 49
    Sivatherium 51
    Toxodon 50
Nautiloids 13, 24
Neanderthals 54, 55
Nema 22
Neural spine
    Carnotaurus 40
    Cryptoclidus 36
    Eryops 33
    Euoplocephalus 43
    Euparkeria 39
    Hoplopteryx 31
    Scaphonyx 39
    Sinokannemeyeria 35
Neusticosaurus pusillus 37
Newts 32
Node 16
Nodule
    Cheiracanthus 30
North America
    Position in Eocene 15
    Position in Jurassic 13
    Position in Middle
        Ordovician 11
Northeast Africa 11
Nose horn core
    Arsinoitherium 15
    Triceratops 42
Nostril notch
    Early tetrapod 33
Nothosaurs 36, 37
Notoungulates 50
Nucleus 9

O

Obturator foramen
    Smilodon 48
Occipital bone
    Hoplophoneus 49
Occipital region
    Cainotherium 51
    Merycoidodon 51
Occiput
    Moeritherium 52
    Phiomia 52
Oceans, formation of 8
Odd-toed ungulates **50–51**
Oil and gas formation 12
Oil formation 10
Old World monkeys 54
Oligocene epoch
    Carnivorous mammals 48
    Elephants 52
    Hoofed mammals 50
    In Cenozoic era 14
    In geological timescale 7
    Primates 54, 55
Opercular bone
    Hoplopteryx 31
Operculum
    Acanthostega 33
    Cheiracanthus 30
Orbit
    Acanthostega 33
    Aegyptopithecus 14, 55
    Archaeopteryx 44
    Arsinoitherium 15
    Benthosuchus 12
    Cainotherium 51
    Compsognathus 41
    Cryptoclidus 37
    Cynognathus 35
    Daphoenus 49
    Dimetrodon 11
    Diplocaulus 32
    Diprotodon 47
    Eryops 32
    Gomphotherium 52
    Homo erectus 55
    Hoplophoneus 49
    Hyaenodon 49
    Ichthyosaurus 13, 37
    Megaloceros 15
    Merycoidodon 51
    Moeritherium 52
    Neanderthal 55
    Neusticosaurus 37
    Parasaurolophus 43
    Phiomia 52
    Phorusrhacus 45
    Protoceratops 42
    Psittacosaurus 42
    Pterodactylus 38
    Rhamphorhynchus 13
    Scaphonyx 39
    Sinokannemeyeria 34
    Sivatherium 51
    Smilodon 49
    Stegoceras 42
    Stegodon 52
    Toxodon 50
    Triceratops 42
Orbital bone
    Bison 51
Ordovician period
    Earliest fishes 28
    In geological timescale 7
    In Paleozoic era 10

Ornithischian dinosaurs
    Compared with
        saurischians 40, 41
    Description **42–43**
Ornithopod dinosaurs 42, 43
Ornithorhynchus 47
Ossicles 27
Ossicone
    Sivatherium 51
Osteichthyes 30, 31
Osteodontornis 44, 45
Ovary
    Flowering plant 21
Ovule
    Cycad 19
    Flowering plant 20, 21
    Gymnosperm 18
Ovuliferous scale 18
Oxygen 8

P

Pachycephalosaurs 42, 43
Painted Desert 7
Paired pectoral fins 28
Paleocene epoch
    Carnivorous mammals 48
    In Cenozoic era 14
    In geological timescale 7
Paleozoic era
    Description **10–11**
    Early fishes 28–31
    In geological timescale 6–7
    Invertebrates 22–27
    Key events **10–11**
Palea 21
Palms 20
Panderichthys 30, 31
Pangaea 10, 11, 12
Papilla 18
Paraceratherium 50
Paranuchal plate 29
Parasaurolophus 42, 43
Parietal bone
    Aegyptopithecus 55
    Cynognathus 35
    Heliobatis 30
    Hesperornis 45
    Homo erectus 55
    Homo rudolfensis 55
    Neanderthal 55
    Osteodontornis 45
Parietal fenestra
    Protoceratops 42
Parietosquamosal frill
    Triceratops 42
Patagopteryx deferrariisi
    44–45
Patella
    Smilodon 48
    Toxodon 51
Pecten beudanti 25
Pectoral fin
    Cephalaspid 28
    Coelacanth 31
    Cheiracanthus 30
    Eusthenopteron 31
    Heliobatis 30
    Hoplopteryx 31
    Panderichthys 31
Pectoral sinus 28
Pedicle valve 25
Peduncle 20
Peloneustes 37
Pelvic clasper 30

Pelvic fin
    Coelacanth 31
    Eusthenopteron 31
    Panderichthys 31
    Heliobatis 30
    Hoplopteryx 31
    Undina 31
Pelvic girdle
    Cryptoclidus 36
    Heliobatis 30
    Lobe-finned fish 31
    Ray-finned fish 31
    Smilodon 48
Pelycosaurs 34, 35
Pennsylvanian period 7
Pentasteria cotteswoldiae 27
Perisore 17
Perissodactyls 50–51
Permian period
    Gymnosperms 18
    In geological timescale 6–7
    In Paleozoic era 8–9
    Temnospondyls 32
Petal 20, 21
Phalanx
    Archaeopteryx 44
    Australopithecus 54
    Compsognathus 41
    Cryptoclidus 36
    Diprotodon 47
    Eryops 32, 33
    Euparkeria 38
    Glyptodon 46, 47
    Neanderthal 47
    Pterodactylus 38
    Scaphonyx 39
    Sinokannemeyeria 34
    Smilodon 48, 49
    Toxodon 50
Phanerozoic eon 6–7
Pharynx
    Coral polyp 23
Phiomia 52, 53
Phorusrhacus inflatus 44, 45
Phragmocone 24
Phylum 56
Pinna
    Ear flap 53
    Leaflet 12
Pinnules 26, 27
Pinus silvestris 18
Pisiform bone 47
Placenta 46
Placentals 46
Placoderms 28
Placodonts 36, 37
Plant kingdom 58
Plasma membrane 9
Platananthus hueberi 21
Platyceras haliotis 25
Platypus 46, 47
Pleistocene epoch
    Elephants and their kin 52
    Hoofed mammals 50
    In Cenozoic era 14, 15
    In geological timescale 7
    Primitive mammals 46
Plesiosaurs 36
Pliocene epoch
    Elephants and their kin 52
    Hoofed mammals 50
    In Cenozoic era 14, 15
    In geological timescale 7
    Primates 54
Pliosaurs 36, 37

Podocarp 19
Polar nuclei 21
Polar view
  Pollen grain 21
Pollen chamber 19
Pollen drop 19
Pollen grains
  Flowering plants 21
  Gymnosperms 18, 19
Pollen tube
  Gymnosperms 18, 19
  Flowering plants 20, 21
Pollen tube nucleus 21
Polychaetes 22, 23
Polycolpites clavatus 21
Poppy pollen 20
Posterior crural muscle
  Patagopteryx 45
Posterior dorsal fin
  Lamprey 29
Posterior femoral muscle
  Carnotaurus 40
  Patagopteryx 45
Posterior ventral lateral
  plate 29
Postesophagus 25
Postfrontal bone
  Ichthyosaurus 37
  Reptilian skulls 35
Postorbital bone
  Aegyptopithecus 14
  Archaeopteryx 45
  Reptilian skulls 35
Postrenal ctenidium
  Chiton 25
Preaxial radial 31
Precambrian time
  Description 8–9
  Echinoderms and
    arthropods 26
  In geological timescale 6
  Time chart 56
Predatory dinosaurs 40, 41
Predentary bone
  Psittacosaurus 42
Prefrontal bone
  Archaeopteryx 45
  Ichthyosaurus 37
  Reptilian skulls 35
Prehistoric time 6–7
Premaxilla
  Archaeopteryx 45
  Bird skulls 45
  Cynognathus 35
  Dimetrodon 11
  Eryops 32
  Gomphotherium 52
  Hesperornis 45
  Ichthyosaurus 37
  Moeritherium 52
  Osteodontornis 45
  Phiomia 52
  Reptilian skulls 35
  Smilodon 49
  Stegodon 52
  Vertebrate skull types 35
Premolar
  Cainotherium 51
  Cynognathus 35
  Hoplophoneus 49
  Hyaenodon 49
  Moeritherium 52
  Phiomia 52
  Toxodon 50
  Ursus 48

Primates 54–55
Primitive fishes 28–29
Primitive mammals 46–47
Primitive plants
  Description 16
  First appearance 10
  Time chart 58
Primitive reptiles 34–35
Proboscideans 52, 53
Progymnosperms 58
Prokaryotes 6, 8–9
Pronephrium asperum 17
Prosauropod dinosaurs 40
Proterozoic aeon
  In geological timescale 6
  In Precambrian time 8–9
Protists
  Animal time chart 56
  Plant time chart 58
  Precambrian time 8
Protoceratops andrewsi 42
Protofagacea allonensis 20
Protozoans 8, 9
Pterichthyodes 28
Pterichthyodes milleri 29
Pteridophytes 16
Pterobranchs 22
Pterocoma pennata 26
Pterodactylus kochi 38
Pterosaurs
  Archosaurs 38
  In Paleozoic era 12, 13
Pubis
  Carnotaurus 41
  Euparkeria 38
  Neanderthal 55
  Ornithischian dinosaur 41
  Patagopteryx 45
  Saurischian dinosaur 41
  Smilodon 48
  Tyrannosaurus 40

Q

Quaternary period
  In Cenozoic era 14, 15
  In geological timescale 6–7

R

Rachis 12, 13
Radial cartilage 30
Radial plate 27
Radius
  Archaeopteryx 44
  Arsinoitherium 15
  Australopithecus 54
  Compsognathus 41
  Diprotodon 47
  Eryops 32
  Euparkeria 39
  Glyptodon 46, 47
  Neanderthal 55
  Patagopteryx 44
  Protoceratops 42
  Pterodactylus 38
  Scaphonyx 39
  Sinokannemeyeria 34
  Smilodon 49
Rancho la Brea tar pit 49
Ray-finned fishes
  Description 30, 31
  Time chart 57
Reproductive duct 43
Reproductive pinnule 26

Reptile postures 34
Reptiles
  Descriptions 34–43
  Mesozoic era 12
  Paleozoic era 10
  Skull types 35
Reticulate surface structure
  Pollen grain 21
Reversed hallux
  Archaeopteryx 44
Rhabdosome 22
Rhamphorhynchus 13
Rhinoceros 50
Rhizome 16
Rhizophore 17
Rhizopoterion cribosum 23
Rhynconellid brachiopod 25
Rhyniophytes 58
Rib
  Bivalve 25
  Brachiopod 25
Ribosomes 9
Rock formations 6
Rose family 20
Rostral bone
  Protoceratops 42
  Psittacosaurus 42
  Triceratops 42
Rostrum 27
Rotularia 22, 23

S

Saber-toothed cat 48–49
Saccus
  Pollen grain 19
Sacrum
  Cryptoclidus 36
  Neanderthal 55
  Smilodon 48
  Toxodon 51
Sagittal crest
  Daphoenus 49
  Hyaenodon 49
  Merycoidodon 51
  Smilodon 49
  Toxodon 50
Sail-backed reptiles 34, 35
Salivary gland 25
Saurischian dinosaurs 40–41
Sauropod dinosaurs 40, 41
Sauropodomorph dinosaurs
  40, 41
Scale leaf 18
Scandinavia, position in
  Middle Ordovician 11
Scaphonyx 39
Scapula
  Archaeopteryx 44
  Arsinoitherium 15
  Carnotaurus 41
  Compsognathus 41
  Cryptoclidus 36
  Diprotodon 47
  Eryops 32
  Euoplocephalus 43
  Euparkeria 38, 39
  Glyptodon 46
  Neusticosaurus 37
  Patagopteryx 45
  Scaphonyx 39
  Sinokannemeyeria 34
  Smilodon 48
  Toxodon 50
Scorpions 26

Scute
  Glyptodon 47
  Minmi 43
Sea anemones 22, 23
Sea lilies 26, 27
Sea reptiles 36, 37
Sea scorpions 26, 57
Sea squirts 23
Sea urchins 26
Seal family 48
Sedimentary rocks 6
Seed ferns
  Description 18
  Time chart 58
Seeds
  Gymnosperms 18, 19
  Flowering plants 20, 21
Selaginella 17
Sensory panel 28
Sepal 28
Septum 23
Serpula 22, 23
Sharks 30
Shoulder girdle
  Eryops 32
Shoulder spike
  Euoplocephalus 43
Shrikes 15
Shrimps 26, 27
Siberia, position in Middle
  Ordovician 11
Sicula 22
Sierra Nevada, uplift of 15
Silurian period
  First spore plants 16
  In geological timescale 7
  In Paleozoic era 10
  Rise of modern fishes 30
Silvianthemum suecicum 20
Single-celled organisms 6
Sinokannemeyeria
  yinchiaoensis 34–35
Siphuncle
  Ammonite 24
  Nautiloid 13
Sivatherium 50, 51
Skull
  Cainotherium 51
  Cynognathus 35
  Early tetrapods 32
  Gomphotherium 52
  Hesperornis 45
  Merycoidodon 51
  Moeritherium 52
  Phiomia 52
  Phorusrhacus 45
  Sivatherium 51
  Stegodon 52–53
Skull openings
  Archosaurs 38
  Reptilian types 34, 35
Skull roof
  Bison 51
Skull shelf
  Stegoceras 42
Slimehead 31
Sloths 46
Small intestine
  Carnotaurus 41
  Euoplocephalus 43
  Euparkeria 39
Smilodon 48–49
Snails 24
Snakes 57
Songbirds 15

South Africa, position in
  Middle Ordovician 11
South America
  Flightless land birds 44–45
  Hoofed mammals 50
  Mammals in Cenozoic 14
  Position in Eocene 15
  Position in Jurassic 13
  Position in Middle
    Ordovician 11
  Primitive mammals 46
Spanomera mauldinensis
  20, 21
Sperm
  Gymnosperms 18
  Flowering plants 20
Spiders 26
Spinal plate 29
Spinosaurus 40
Spiny anteaters 46
Spiny sharks 30
Spiracle 33
Spiracular gill chamber 28
Sponges
  Description 22, 23
  Paleozoic era 10
  Time chart 56
Sporangiophore 16
Sporangium 16, 17, 19
Spore-bearing plants 16–17
Spores 16, 17
Sporophyll 17, 19
Sporophyte 16, 17
Sprawling gait 34
Squamosal bone
  Aegyptopithecus 14
  Eryops 32
  Reptilian skulls 35
  Stegodon 52
  Vertebrate skulls 33
Stamen 20
Starfishes 26, 27
Stegoceras 42
Stegodon 52–53
Stegosaurs 42, 43
Sternum
  Smilodon 48
  Toxodon 50
Stigma 21
Stomach
  Euparkeria 39
Strobilus 16
Stromatolite 9
Style 20, 21
Submarginal plate 29
Sugar gland 25
Superkingdoms 8
Surface sculpturing 33
Suture 24
Swim bladders 30
Sycamore family 21
Synapsid reptiles 34–35
Synapsid skull 35

T

Tabula 23
Tabular bone
  Eryops 32
Tail bones
  Pterodactylus 38
Tail club
  Euoplocephalus 42
Tail crest
  Acanthostega 33

Tail fan
  Shrimp 27
Tail feather
  Archaeopteryx 44
  Patagopteryx 45
Tail shield
  Trilobite 27
Tail spine
  Stingray 30
Tail vertebra
  Stingray 30
Tar pit 49
Tarsal bone
  Cryptoclidus 36
Tarsometatarsal
  Patagopteryx 45
Temnospondyls
  Description 32
  Time chart 57
Tendon
  Patagopteryx 45
Tentacles
  Ammonite 24
  Belemnite 24
  Coral polyp 23
Tepal 20
Tertiary period
  Birds 44
  Grasses 20
  In Cenozoic era 14–15
  In geological timescale 6–7
  Mammals 46–55
Tetrapods
  In rise of amphibians 32
  Paleozoic era 10, 11
  Westlothiana lizziae 34
Thalloid liverwort 16
Thallus
  Liverwort 16
Theca
  Graptolite 22
Thecal aperture 22
Thecodonts 38–39
Therapsids 34, 35
Theria 46

Theropod dinosaurs
  Description 40, 41
  In evolution of birds 44
Thoracic vertebra 39
Thorax 27
Thyestes 28
Thyreophorans 42, 43
Tibia
  Archaeopteryx 44
  Arsinoitherium 15
  Australopithecus 54
  Compsognathus 41
  Diprotodon 47
  Eryops 32
  Euparkeria 38
  Glyptodon 46
  Lobe-finned fish 31
  Neusticosaurus 37
  Pterodactylus 38
  Ray-finned fish 31
  Scaphonyx 39
  Sinokannemeyeria 35
  Smilodon 48
  Tyrannosaurus 40
Tibiotarsus 45
Tine 15
Toads 32
Toxodon platensis 50–51
Trachea 41
Trachyphyllia chipolana 23
Tremataspis 28
Triassic period
  Archosaurs 38
  Dinosaurs 40
  In geological timescale 6–7
  In Mesozoic era 12
  Marine reptiles 36
  Primitive reptiles 34
Triceratops 42
Trichome 20
Triconodonts 46
Trigonocarpus adamsi 18
Trilobites
  Description 26, 27
  Time chart 56, 57

Trunk
  Mammuthus primigenius 53
Tube feet 26, 27
Tuber 16
Tubercle 26
Tuojiangosaurus 42
Turtles
  Evolution 36
  Time chart 57
Tusks
  Arthrodire 29
  Gomphotherium 52
  Loxodonta 53
  Phiomia 52, 53
  Sinokannemeyeria 34
  Stegodon 53
  Woolly mammoth 52–53
Tyrannosaurus rex 40

U

Ulna
  Archaeopteryx 44
  Arsinoitherium 15
  Australopithecus 54
  Compsognathus 41
  Diprotodon 47
  Eryops 32
  Euoplocephalus 43
  Euparkeria 38
  Glyptodon 46, 47
  Neanderthal 55
  Patagopteryx 44
  Protoceratops 42
  Pterodactylus 38
  Scaphonyx 39
  Sinokannemeyeria 34
  Smilodon 49
Umbilicus
  Ammonite shell 24
  Nautiloid shells 10, 13
Umbo 25
Underhair
  Mammuthus primigenius 53
Undina penicillata 31

Ungulate
  Description 50–51
  Pleistocene example 15
Upper incisor
  Cainotherium 51
  Hoplophoneus 49
Ureter
  Euoplocephalus 43

V

Valves
  Mollusk shells 25
Vascular plants 16
Vascular structure 17
Velar ridge 28
Velvet worms 22
Venter 10
Ventral antibrachial muscle
  Euoplocephalus 43
Ventral intermediate spines
  Cheiracanthus 30
Ventral scale 28
Vertebra
  Coelacanth 31
  Hominid 54
  Stingray 30
Vertebral column
  Hoplopteryx 31
Vertebral projection
  Edaphosaurus 35
Vertebrates
  Earliest 28
  Time chart 56
Vestibule
  Cephalaspid skull 28
Virgella 22
Volcanoes 8

W

Water-exhalant chamber
  Chiton 25
Water-exhalant slits
  Carpoid 26

Water-inhalant chamber
  Chiton 25
Watertight eggs
  Amniotes 34
Weasel family 48
Westlothiana lizziae 34
Whales
  In Cenozoic era 14
  Ancestry 48
Whorl
  Mollusk shell 25
Wing feather
  Archaeopteryx 44
Winged insects 10
Woolly mammoth 52–53
Woolly rhinoceros 50
World climate 10
Worms
  Early Cambrian 10
  Polychaete 22, 23
  Velvet 22

X

Xystridura saint-smithii 27

Z

Zion Canyon 6
Zooid
  Graptolite 22
Zosterophyll 58
Zygomatic arch
  Glyptodon 47
  Hyaenodon 49
  Merycoidodon 51
  Moeritherium 52
  Smilodon 49
  Stegodon 52
  Toxodon 50
Zygomatic bone
  Aegyptopithecus 55
  Homo erectus 55
  Homo rudolfensis 55
  Neanderthal 55

Acknowledgments

Research, advice, and assistance
Madeline Harley for advice and editorial help on
fossil pollen 16–21; Marie Kurmann for advice and
editorial help on fossil spores and on gymnosperm
pollen 16–19; Darrin Dooling for assistance with
photography of living *Equisetum giganteum* 16,
Pronephrium asperum 17, and cycad cones 19; Alan
Hemsley for advice and editorial help on plants 16–
21 and plant time chart 58; Pat Herendeen, Else
Marie Friis, and Joseph R. Thomasson for editorial
help on flowering plants 20–21; Sue Rigby for advice
and editorial help on graptolites 22; Douglas Palmer
for advice and editorial help on graptolites and
corals 22–23 and animal time chart 56–57; Jenny
Clack for advice and editorial help on amphibians
32–33, for research on model of *Acanthostega
gunnari* 33, and for help, with Elizabeth Hide, on
animal time chart 56–57; Michael Coates for advice
on classification and for research on *Acanthostega*
model 33; Richard Hammond for artwork reference
and advice on *Euparkeria capensis* 38–39; and Colin
Harrison for advice on birds 44–45.

Makers or owners of models shown in this book
Roby Braun: *Carnotaurus sastrei* 1, 40–41; John
Holmes: *Hyracotherium* 5, 49, *Westlothiana lizziae* 3,

34, and *Euoplocephalus tutus* 42–43; Richard
Hammond and University Museum, Oxford:
Acanthostega gunnari 33; Royal Scottish Museum:
Aglaophyton 16; Natural History Museum, London:
Cothurnocystis eliziae 26, *Archaeopteryx* 44, and
Smilodon 48; and Royal British Columbia Museum,
Victoria, Canada: woolly mammoth 52–53.

 Model of starfish, p. 27, by Somso-
Modelle, Coburg, Germany.

**Picture agencies and individuals who have
provided photographs for this book**
(Abbreviations: t top, b bottom, l left, r right,
c center, a above)
Department of Library Services, American Museum
of Natural History/D. Finnin/C. Chesek (negative
no. 4936/3) 54bl; Cleveland Museum of Natural
History 29br; Simon Conway Morris 22tl; Else Marie
Friis 20tr, cr, bl, 21bc; David George 23tr; Pat
Herendeen 20bla, bc, br, 21cl, bl; Andrew H. Knoll
8tr, 9bc,br; Ligabue Studies and Research Center
Archive, Venice 42bl; Natural History Museum,
London 44bl, 46–47b, 48b; OSF/G. I Bernard 28tl;
Douglas Palmer 22br; Sue Rigby 22bl, 22bc; Royal
Botanic Gardens, Kew 16cr, 17cla, cl, clb, 18br, bc,

19bl, bc, 21c; Science Photo Library/ Walter Alvarez
6bl, Jeremy Burgess 20tl; Thomas N. Taylor 17tl; and
Joseph R. Thomasson 21tl.

**Museums that have kindly given permission for
Dorling Kindersley to take photographs**
University Museum, Oxford; Hunterian Museum,
Glasgow University; Natural History Museum,
London; Royal Scottish Museum, Edinburgh;
Yorkshire Museum; Queensland Museum, South
Brisbane; Royal British Columbia Museum, Victoria;
Royal Tyrrell Museum of Paleontology, Alberta;
Naturmuseum Senckenberg, Frankfurt; and Institut
und Museum für Geologie und Paläontologie der
Universität Tübingen; *Acanthostega gunnari* skull on
p. 33 was photographed at the Zoology Museum,
Cambridge while on loan from the Geological
Museum, Copenhagen.

Dorling Kindersley photographers
Andy Crawford, Steve Gorton, and Sarah Ashun.

Additional illustrators
Selwyn Hutchinson, Alison Ellis, Mei Lim, Alex
Pang, and Ingegerd Svensson (principal illustrators
are credited separately on p. 4).